TAILS ON THE WING

ROBERT PLANT

BETHCAR PUBLICATIONS

ISBN 978-1-7398528-2-5

31 Carragh Road, Bushmills, Co. Antrim, BT57 8UE

Scripture references are taken from The Holy Bible (KJV)

Printed and designed by Michelle McCabe 07787 586693

To

CYNTHIA HORSFALL

in grateful appreciation of your
friendship, faithfulness to truth and editing efforts
on previous books and compilations.

She hath been a succourer of many,
and of myself also.
(Romans Ch16 v2)

Red Kite

CONTENTS

ACKNOWLEDGEMENTS

Any book requires the help of others, and this little volume is no exception. I am indebted to my wife, Karen, for the many hours of dedicated work she has put into ensuring the contents are readable in their present form.

Rhoda Dover from Dublin also expanded much time and effort proofreading and making helpful suggestions to the original text for which the book is much richer.

I thank Ernest Dover for first asking me to conduct children's meetings on Zoom for the Rathmines Gospel Hall, Dublin, during the first covid lockdown in 2020. Ernest also encouraged me to use my knowledge of wildlife to interest listeners in the greater message of the Gospel, which then inspired me to write this book. Thank you too, Ernest, for kindly supplying the Foreword.

Michelle McCabe of Antrim has done an outstanding job in typesetting and designing the cover and contents. Her patience, especially when my wife Karen and I decided on a second edit, was much appreciated.

I ask the reader's forgiveness for the somewhat poor photos used in this publication. I am, after all, a Gospel preacher, not a wildlife photographer. I have neither the time nor equipment to obtain the quality material that a book on wildlife and the subjects themselves deserve.

For those chapters where I could not provide my own images, I thankfully acknowledge the following for kindly allowing me to use their excellent and professional material:

Ian Dickey - Cuckoo (Page 37)

Garry Wilkinson - Cuckoo being fed by Meadow Pipit (Page 38)

Chris Mason - Shrew (Page 44)

John Parkinson - Buzzards (Page 128 and 132)

Garry Wilkinson - Slavonian Grebe (Page 143)

I'm also very grateful to Jim Wells for assisting in my efforts to obtain such suitable photographs.

Without the willing assistance of all these people, this publication would be much the poorer.

Stoat

FOREWORD

In March 2020, a sickness, a plague we never knew before, arrived, migrating worldwide from a place we had never heard of, bringing dangers and restrictions we had never imagined.

We all learned new words like Coronavirus, social distancing, lockdown and about working and schooling from home. Stay at home was the law.

The Scriptures tell us how important it is to teach and learn from God's Word; ***"And that from a child thou hast known the holy scriptures, which are able to make thee wise unto salvation through faith which is in Christ Jesus."*** Also, it is important to see and encourage one another and not remain in complete isolation.

Listening to and seeing visiting speakers over 'Zoom' gave us a daily focus, encouragement, and uplift for young and old, as was meeting those from near and far, logging in from every continent.

In April 2020, Robert Plant was likely the first to conduct a children's series over Zoom, illustrated by his fascinating knowledge and collection of birds and animals.

These stories told during lockdown, exalting the Creator, and telling of the Saviour, form the basis of this beautifully illustrated book, which I commend for the blessing of our children and grandchildren.

Ernest Dover
Rathmines, Dublin.

Puffin

INTRODUCTION

Wildlife! It's fascinating, whether it's the humble sparrow most of us see daily, one of the more exotic-looking birds that sometimes cross our path, the tiny house mouse or the impressively powerful badger. They are all to be admired.

Wildlife and looking after it has always been a part of my life. In a previous home, we had four hedgehog boxes in the garden and would occasionally help out the local hedgehog hospital by reintroducing recovered hedgehogs to the wild.

All of us in the family remember when we tried to help a sick hedgehog we named 'Haley'. The poor thing was desperately underweight. For a week, we kept her warm, fed and watered in the garage under the supervision of Theresa from our local hedgehog rescue centre. Sadly, some animals and birds choose death rather than life, and no matter how hard we try or what efforts we take to save them, we will fail. Such was the case with Haley. On the seventh night of care, I saw she had given up the will to live, with a bit of persuasion, my wife, Karen, allowed me to bring her into our utility room so that she was easier to watch.

I clambered out of bed at one o'clock in the morning to check on the poor thing. Haley's breathing was shallow, and she was unresponsive despite earnest entreaties for her to think again and choose life. The following day Haley was lying lifeless in the wooden crate we had kept her in. We were somewhat devastated. Our daughter came down for breakfast and asked what was wrong. When I told her that Haley had died, her response was simple.

"We did all we could for her dad; at least she died loved and cared for."

She was right. We couldn't have done any more. We buried Haley in our garden and purchased a small ornamental hedgehog, which I inscribed underneath with Haley's name and the date she died. I'm funny that way; even our dogs 'Barney' and 'Wellington' are buried in our garden with little headstones recording their names and dates of birth and death, along with 'Fluffy', our pet rabbit.

We had humane animal traps even for the pests in the garage or garden, and these allowed us to see the wonders of God's unique creation close up whenever we caught something. There was the mole, whose powerful front claws tore through the fabric of a pair of leather welding gloves. We also captured an angry and antagonistic grey squirrel who wanted to bite us as we tried to release him. We caught the mice in the garage, all of which we would have loved to keep as pets, and the odd bird, which issued warning calls before flying unharmed away.

I also used these traps to try and catch a hedgehog that I had seen while walking the dogs one freezing, snowy week at the end of November. It was obviously sick as it should have been hibernating. The area where we had initially found it was at the far end of our housing estate. This venture saw me wandering through the snow in my wellington boots and a coat covering my pyjamas in the dark hours of the night. I wondered if any of the neighbours saw me on these nocturnal trips! Unfortunately, the hedgehog never took the bait in the traps, and I can only imagine it did not survive the cold winter months.

I suppose most children would find it a little odd, to say the least, when their father came home and walked through the front door of his suburban house dressed in a suit with a wild duck under his arm! I had initially seen it on my way to a meeting. Three hours later, the poor thing was still sitting in the same position on the side of the road. The rain was teeming down. I had neglected to take a coat but undeterred and dressed in my navy blue suit, white shirt, smart tie and best shoes, I leapt out of the car and, after chasing the duck for some distance along a footpath, managed to corner it, catch it and get it into my vehicle.

Of course, ducks, especially wild ones, are not like dogs. They don't sit still when told or lie down on command. Thankfully I was not too far from home, so the battle between soaking duck and safe driving was only a short one. Afterwards, the car required a thorough scrubbing, and my suit had to be taken to the dry cleaners while the duck took up happy residence in our back garden, scaring the fish witless that lived in our tiny pond.

Eventually, we placed an advert in the local paper seeking a more suitable abode for Jemima as we had named her after the Beatrix Potter character Jemima Puddle-Duck. A man who owned a large house less than a mile away, with a massive lake and other similar ducks, kindly offered her a home. From the way she left my arms to dive into his pond, you could say she took to her new home like... well, a duck to water!

No one in the family has ever fully understood why spiders who visit our house for shelter must be preserved at all costs. If I find a spider at home, I will never harm it; they are such valuable members of the insect family, catching and killing much less desirable visitors. Sadly, because of their eight legs and strange way of running, many people have a phobia about them that results in them tragically falling victim to a folded magazine or the sole of a shoe. Spiders are a vital food source for many native birds, such as robins, tits and wrens, to name just three. Much better, therefore, to catch them and place them back outside the house. We have a handy little thing called a 'spider vac', which is used to remove many an intrepid eight legged explorer.

There is also my habit of stopping the car with a squeal of brakes, leaping out like a police officer about to make an arrest, only to draw out my camera and take a photo of something I have spotted as I have been driving along. Such behaviour, of course, is not to be undertaken on a busy motorway or any busy road for that matter!

Then there are the walks we go on. As well as boots, leads and dogs, into the car must go camera, binoculars, and a large-brimmed hat – if you are a serious birdwatcher, you must look the part! If we are going on holiday, add to that list telescope and tripod.

I can guarantee that a lesser spotted pink-legged red-breasted sawbilled buzzard owl will turn up when I do not have my camera. Okay, okay, there is no such bird, at least I have never heard of one, but you get the idea. If you don't go prepared, you don't see what's around. Often both my wife and daughter would become exasperated on a walk as they look back to see me trailing in the distance, or with the camera to my eye, taking the five hundred and sixty-seventh photo of a stonechat!

This book is an introduction to the sometimes crazy world of the birdwatcher. It has, though, been written to be more than that – much more. Throughout its pages, I hope you learn not just about birds – and the occasional mammal – but about God, His Word, His Son and His will for you. These are the vitally important things in life. The Lord Jesus told His disciples to, ***'Behold the fowls of the air'*** ***(Matthew 6:26).*** 'Behold' means taking a good look at, learning from, thinking about and considering seriously. As you read these pages, I trust that you may learn about these various exciting creatures and, more importantly, discover more incredible things that God desires to teach you.

Little Owl

GRIPPING GREY HERONS
– LONG NECKS AND SHARP BEAKS

Fascinating Facts
Despite their size, herons usually nest relatively high up in trees and often steal material from other heron's nests to help construct their own. Their curved necks are used like a spring, propelling the head forward so they can spear a passing fish on their lower mandible before throwing it in the air, catching it and swallowing it head first.

What is it about this bird that makes you want to say 'wow' every time you see it? Perhaps it is its mighty wingspan which is well over one and a half metres. Then again, it might be its size, standing with its neck extended over a metre high. Of course, if you look at that long neck that can easily bend into the letter 'S' shape, you must be impressed.

Another glance will observe its impressively long slender legs that seem almost too thin to hold its bulky body upright. However, the heron's most captivating feature is its long powerful yellow dagger-like beak, ideal for catching fish and other unfortunate creatures upon which it wishes to feast from the water or bank-side. All in all, the heron is a very striking bird.

Thankfully it is not too difficult to find as long as you look for it near water. You can spot a heron standing alongside slow meandering rivers, fast-flowing streams, on the banks of reservoirs and lakes, and along the seashore. Take a look anywhere that you think Mr or Mrs Heron might decide to stop to have breakfast, lunch or dinner!

Many years ago, as a family, we had gone away to Stowmarket in Suffolk to take a week of children's meetings. The meetings were conducted in the morning during the Easter school holidays, leaving the afternoons free to explore the area. On one of these days, we took a trip to the Norfolk Broads, a place of extensive wetlands and mudflats ideal for seeing a lot of wildlife.

Once there, we soon decided to hire a motorboat for a couple of hours.

I would like to think that I am a half-decent driver nearly forty years after passing my driving test. However, my ability to handle a boat with a motor, albeit a very slow one, turned out to be quite different.

As we reversed out of the area where the boats were berthed, the one we were given seemed to have a mind of its own. We bashed into the other floating vessels in what appeared to be a futile attempt to get free and onto the open water. The owner rather frantically kept calling instructions to me from the shore as he, no doubt, contemplated the destruction of his entire fleet.

Finally, having discovered that reversing a boat is like reversing a car with a trailer, we were free and onto the open water. As we motored slowly away, my hot and flustered face began to return from a bright beetroot red to its usual colour! It was a relief to get away from the stony gaze of the frowning owner and one or two other spectators.

Once up to full power - a snail-paced two miles an hour! We throttled out among the reed-beds. Here we saw dabbling ducks amongst lots of pondweed and many other birds stupid enough not to take flight at the approach of the crawling vessel with the novice captain at the helm.

We timed our trip an hour out, then turned around for an hour back. Upon our return, we entered a small channel running alongside a low wall. Halfway along the wall and overlooking the water stood a splendid-looking grey heron, seemingly totally unphased by the approach of our craft.

As we drew nearer, it still did not fly away in fright, so I suggested to Karen that she got my camera and took a photo.

She picked the camera bag off the deck to extract the camera. At the same instant, the heron jumped off the wall into the water directly in front of the boat. Seconds later, it was back on the wall with a giant flatfish held tightly and proudly in its beak.

"Quick," I called in desperation as I saw the excellent photo opportunity reveal itself before our eyes, "take a photo!"

"How do I turn it on?" Karen enquired as the heron toyed with its catch to ensure it went down the right way.

"Red button on the top," I called as I throttled the boat back to idle to avoid getting too close.

"Which red button?"

"That one!" I replied as I saw the giant fish head down in its captor's beak.

"Now, what do I do?"

"Point it and take the photo," I responded as the giant fish began to descend from beak to throat.

My visions of the photo winning the 'Wildlife Photographer of the Year' competition began to evaporate as quickly as the unfortunate fish was itself disappearing.

"What do I do to take the photo?"

"Press that button on the top right!"

"This one?"

"Yes, that one," I answered as patiently as possible as the fish slipped silently out of sight to its final doom in the heron's stomach.

"Okay. Oh!" my wife responded as the heron took flight and majestically flew away, "It's gone!"

It seemed that as it climbed into the sky, the heron was smugly saying, 'I gave you a chance to take the photo of a lifetime, but you were not ready.'

To the total surprise of the boat owner, we sailed back into the mooring area and parked the boat without all the palaver and chaos we had experienced on the way out. The fact that a hot and bothered father, a little annoyed at seeing such a magnificent photo opportunity lost, had been replaced at the helm by his twelve-year-old daughter just maybe had something to do with our safe arrival back at port!

There had been a fantastic opportunity for us as a family to obtain a wonderful photo of a grey heron eating its dinner. We missed it; however, today, as you read this book, there is a great opportunity for you to be saved. Every day God waits, and He says, ***'Now is the accepted time; behold, now is the day of salvation'*** ***(2nd Corinthians Ch6 v2).***

The Lord Jesus, God's Son, died on the cross, finished the work of salvation, paid the price for your sin and rose again. There is nothing for you to do but repent of your sin and trust Him as Saviour.

All we missed was a photo; however, without trusting Christ as Saviour, you will miss Heaven!

WAGGING WAGTAILS
– THE BIRDS WITH WAGGLY TAILS

Female Grey Wagtail

Fascinating Facts
Female pied wagtails build their nests without male assistance, and they can sometimes be made in unusual places such as old disused cars. While the female creates the nest, the male follows its mate, chirping encouragement. In winter, they can form enormous flocks to help keep each other warm.

There is something lovely about the busy little grey wagtail, which can be found along fast-flowing rivers and streams. Perhaps it is its habit of continually wagging its tail up and down, almost bobbing, as it moves quickly across stones and rocks dotted along some babbling brook.

I perhaps have an affection for this beautiful little bird because of its colour scheme. The contrast of its grey head and back with its yellow breast and rump makes it stand out from the crowd. In Britain and Ireland, we have three main species of wagtail; the pied, the grey and the yellow.

Stop and look at any wagtail you see, and it will be evident how they obtained the name; they all have the same characteristic of wagging their tails in that up and down motion – they never cease – it's continuous. Experts inform us that a dog tells you that it is happy by swishing its tail from side to side, but never up and down like a wagtail.

Often, the wagtail will suddenly take off, flutter a metre or so into the air and return close to where it was before. This behaviour is repeated time and time again as they spot a juicy fly passing by and leap to grab it. Food is the prime focus of most birds, and obtaining enough to keep them alive, especially in winter, is a continual battle.

In the introduction, I mentioned trying never to leave my camera behind. I remember an occasion doing just that one Saturday afternoon. Karen wanted to pop into the local butchers and supermarket for some provisions. Unusually there was nowhere to park on the main street, so we pulled into a small car park that overlooks the river. As Karen went off to obtain the required items, I decided to wander along the river bank.

I had just closed the car door when I saw it; a grey wagtail was sitting on a large rock bobbing up and down in the middle of the swollen river less than twenty metres from me! It was beautiful, with vivid grey, yellow, and white colours. I went to get my camera and then remembered it wasn't there. This gorgeous little bird in a beautiful location was right in front of me, sitting up, almost asking to be photographed, and I could not do so simply because I had not prepared before leaving home! It was exasperating.

On another occasion, I had been shopping in the local town with Karen, and for some reason that I have now forgotten, she had to move the car, so she drove it to Tesco car park, where we agreed to meet. I arrived before she did, and having no key, I had to 'stand about' trying my hardest not to look too suspicious as the minutes seemed like hours!

Thankfully a little pied wagtail appeared and began flitting between cars, searching for something to eat. You will often see pied wagtails in supermarket car parks; they know that little titbits can be left by shoppers returning to their vehicles laden with food. On this particular day, I enjoyed the antics of this little visitor chasing around; it was amazing just how alert it was to danger. At a car's approach, it seemed to wait until almost the last second before taking off with its see-saw flight to land safely a few metres away. It continued this behaviour

Pied Wagtail

repeatedly while cars, trolleys, and pedestrians passed. The little pied wagtail was ever on the lookout, ready in an instant to flee when it perceived danger coming.

Two spaces away from me, a dark-coloured Skoda pulled in, and I was surprised to see two police officers in full uniform get out. It was an unmarked police car!

'Someone's reported me acting suspiciously around these cars in the car park,' I thought as they approached me.

"Morning," one said as he drew level with me.

"Good morning," I answered cheerily and as innocent-sounding as possible.

The two officers carried on walking past me and into Tesco. Was I ever relieved?

A few minutes later, they returned carrying a bag that obviously contained their lunch.

They passed me again and climbed back into their car, the engine started, and the driver began reversing out of his parking space just as a little older man in a bright yellow vehicle drew alongside the rear of the police car.

'BANG!' The police car backed straight into the side of the yellow vehicle.

The poor elderly driver was understandably very upset and shocked at being side-swiped by the Skoda. Then as the police officer re-parked his car, and both he and his colleague got out, his face turned from shock to utter disbelief and fear. Maybe the dear man had visions of being arrested, tried and carted off to prison for attempting to find a parking space in a Tesco car park; I don't know! As it was, the two policemen were very apologetic towards the poor motorist, ensuring he was alright and even offering to get him a drink from the supermarket. As with all accidents involving police vehicles, nothing could be done until an inspector had arrived to examine the scene and make a report.

As they waited for the inspector's arrival, I wandered over to the driver of the yellow car.

"I'm sure you won't have any problem with these men," I said, pointing in the direction of the two embarrassed police officers, "but I did see all that happened if you require a witness."

"Thank you," the driver responded, "I appreciate that, it was quite a shock."

"I can imagine it was," I consoled, "but it will be a good story to tell the family when you get back home."

The driver chuckled as one of the police officers came up to me.

"I guess I'd better take your particulars, sir, as you witnessed it."

As I provided my name and address, I added, "You know I have the highest regard for all that you do, I always wanted to join the force myself. I must say, though, it was rather comical to see your colleague make such a basic driving error!"

The policeman stopped writing and chuckled, "It just shows that none of us is perfect!"

I had to agree with that. No one is perfect except, of course, the Lord Jesus.

We can learn from the police officers that whoever we are, and however long we have been on the Christian pathway, it is essential to be careful. The pied wagtail was alert and off and away long before the danger from a vehicle or shopper came too close.

Male Grey Wagtail

Danger can be all around; it can come in the form of temptation from our friends to join them in something we know is wrong or watching or looking at things on the computer it would be better not to see. Admiring people who lead lives without any thought for God or drinking or eating something we know could harm our bodies are all things it is better to avoid. Try to be alert to the dangers around you and be off and away like the pied wagtail before they can harm you.

When I saw the grey wagtail in our local river, I had not prepared properly before leaving home and, as a result, missed a great photo opportunity. Daily we need to prepare for everything that will come our way. A Christian does this by reading their Bible and spending time in prayer. The Psalmist says***, 'I cry unto thee daily'*** ***(Psalm 86 v33)*** and ***'Thy Word have I hid in my heart that I might not sin against Thee,'*** ***(Psalm 119 v11),*** remember, too, that Satan trembles every time he sees a Christian on his knees.

The poor police officer let his concentration slip for just a moment and bumped into another car. When we neglect these two vitally important daily habits of praying and reading our Bibles, we are more likely to be careless and fail the Lord.

WACKY WRENS
– THE TINY BANDIT

Fascinating Facts
The female can lay up to nine eggs and incubates them all herself; however, the male helps feed the chicks once the eggs have hatched. The Scottish islands hold several subspecies of wren that have longer tails and wings but shorter beaks than their mainland cousins. The image of a wren appeared on Britain's smallest coin called a farthing.

Considering that the wren is the most abundant bird in the United Kingdom, it can be surprisingly tricky to find. It is tiny in the extreme and is often only spotted as it darts across a path like a little brown ball propelled through the air by rubber band fuelled wings. These beat so fast that you wonder how such a small creature can keep up such a hectic pace.

Often as we are walking our dogs along the cliff paths close to home, we hear the '*chat, chat, chat, chat, chat*' call of the wren in the bushes nearby, a bit like the sound of a bandit in ambush firing off a round of ammunition from a machine gun.

The wren is a restless bird dashing here and there, searching for a grub, spider, caterpillar or beetle to carry off to its nest to feed its little family.

I first became properly acquainted with the tiny wren just after Karen and I were married. We lived in a rather unusual modern terraced house with two stories at the front but three at the rear, with the garage underneath. It was a great starter home.

There was a set of stone steps at the back which led from the garage to the kitchen door, and underneath them was a sheltered place where we kept our rubbish bin.

One day as I opened the back door, I was surprised to see a wren scooting off with its warning 'tic tic' call; it was clearly disturbed by my sudden and no doubt noisy appearance. As I watched, it landed on a nearby bush, waited for a second and then flew back under the steps from where it had come.

I cautiously looked below the concrete stairs and saw a wren's delicate nest carefully placed on a couple of overhanging bricks used in constructing the steps. How excited and how amazed I was. We had not been aware of what had been taking place for some days right under our feet.

As I read about the wren, I was surprised to discover the male can build up to seven nests before courting a female. She then chooses which she prefers. I wondered, would the chosen nest be ours under our back steps? I waited anxiously until the whir of tiny wings and the little birds' constant activity told me our nest was the chosen one. Karen and I looked in daily as the female sat on the nest, incubating the eggs.

On one occasion, I noticed a neighbour boy from several houses away taking an unusual interest in the activities below my steps. A day later, I looked out to see him approaching with a stick in his hand. I was worried about what he was going to do.

I quickly opened the back door, "You're not doing anything you shouldn't?" I asked pointedly.

Hastily trying to hide the stick behind his back, the boy replied, "Errr, No!"

"Good!" I responded, "You see, there is a pair of wrens nesting under my steps, and I don't want anything to happen to them, the eggs or the babies. Will you keep an eye out and bang my door if you see any cats or people you think may harm them?"

I hoped that by getting him to help me look after them, he would no longer have any desire to poke at them with a stick or whatever he had been planning on doing.

He agreed, and, having shown him the nest with the female sitting there, the danger I felt he posed was averted.

One Tuesday evening, as we prepared to leave and go to the mid-week prayer and Bible teaching meeting, we heard both parent birds sitting on our fence, making a great commotion. I dashed out to see what was the matter, fearing that someone or something was attacking the nest containing the young feathered birds.

Wren

I soon realised that the parent birds were calling the fledgelings out of the nest as the babies were now old enough to fly. I quietly returned inside and stood at our dining room window with Karen, watching this incredible scene unfold. Slowly, nervously and somewhat ungainly, the young birds emerged one at a time to join the parents on our fence. As we watched, we had one eye on the wrens and another on our watches as time ticked away, we didn't want to be late for the meeting. We hoped to see all the babies emerge unscathed before we left.

We did – just! We arrived at the Bible teaching meeting with a minute to spare, thrilled at the sight we had just witnessed.

We all enjoy the thrill of a new life — the baby brother, sister, cousin, niece or nephew or perhaps the newborn puppy or kitten. All of them are exciting, all with the possibility of doing something extraordinary when they are grown.

The Bible speaks about being '***born again***' **(John Ch3 v7),** a rather strange term that means we are made fit for Heaven. When we are born into the world, we are fitted for this environment with lungs to breathe, eyes to see, ears to hear, and limbs to use. Sadly, because of our sin, we are not fit for Heaven, a place of holiness. To be made ready for that place, we must be *born again*. This occurs when we understand that our sin is a serious problem to God keeping us out of Heaven, and we trust Christ as our Saviour.

When we are *born again,* God gives us new life and a new nature that allows us to think beyond the things of this passing world to those of Heaven. The Bible states, ***'Therefore if any man be in Christ, he is a new creature: old things are passed away; behold, all things are become new'*** **(2nd Corinthians Ch5 v17).** Like those little wrens, we become no longer earthbound because we will have heavenly goals and desires, no longer wanting to please ourselves but having a desire to please God and to be kind to others.

Which realm are you living for, earth or Heaven?

CAPTIVATING CHAFFINCHES
– COMMON AND COLOURFUL CHARACTERS

Fascinating Facts
A singing chaffinch might repeat his song up to three thousand times a day. Due to their singing abilities, the Victorians used to trap and cage them and even enter them in singing competitions. In pre-mechanical times chaffinches stayed close to threshing floors where the seed was removed from the kernel. They would search among the 'chaff' (the waste) for seeds that had been missed. This behaviour gave rise to its name 'chaff-finch'.

It seems a shame that because the chaffinch is such a common little bird, it is often overlooked, even in the garden, as people only notice the larger or seemingly more attractive birds.

Take a look at the humble chaffinch, preferably if you can, through a pair of binoculars. Notice that russet red plumage of the male and that incredibly detailed grey hood that comes from its neck over the back of the head rather like a hoodie. Don't miss that little black part across the forehead and down to the beak.

Now, observe its wings with the lovely patterning of grey, black and white topped off with a bit of yellow along the wing bars. The chaffinch is a bird that should capture anyone's imagination with its many varied colours.

If you get the opportunity, try to listen to its wonderful song and see if you think it sounds like it is mocking you. It sort of laughs first and

Chaffinch eating out of the hand

then adds the surprise element. It is far better to hear bird songs rather than try to explain them, but the chaffinch sort of goes, 'Ha, ha, ha, ha, I shot you!'

Just after Karen and I were married, we had a two-week holiday in Scotland, staying on the shores of Loch Ruthven, known for its splendid but rare slavonian grebes. It was an enjoyable holiday in many ways as I saw my first osprey and came face-to-face, as far as I can remember, for the first time with the lovely little siskin.

One day we decided to travel to the other side of Loch Ness to visit Drumnadrochit, the famous Urquhart Castle and Glen Affric. As soon as we parked in the car park at Glen Affric, we noticed several people holding out their hands and, amazingly, chaffinches landing on them and eating out of them.

We immediately broke bread off our sandwiches and tried holding it out in our open hands. In no time, tiny sharp feet landed, lightly gripping our hands as the birds took full advantage of the crumbs offered. We were thrilled to hold such beautiful and delicate birds in our hands as they gladly accepted the food.

Many years later, we returned with our daughter hoping to recapture that visit and have the chaffinches feed on our hands again. Sadly it was a different time of year, and not only did the chaffinches not feed, but they were also tricky to spot at all.

Thankfully we have several visiting the bird table daily, vying for the seeds and nuts we have on offer. Some can be pretty pushy, chasing off other species and even other chaffinches as they attempt to keep the food for themselves. I always find their antics and interaction with other birds fun to watch, and I often remember that fantastic day when wild birds fed from our hands.

We all need to eat. It is vital for life. A friend of ours used to say to the children who weren't eating their dinners, "Come on, you need to eat up; otherwise, you will grow skinny and die!"

He was right; we need to eat and eat the right kinds of food to stay healthy. It is vital and just the same in the Christian life. If we continually feed our minds off the television, our computers, the internet or any other manner of distractions, our Christian life will soon be in trouble. We need the proper diet to keep right with God. Philippians ch.4 in the Bible tells us to think about those things which are good, true, pure and lovely. Nature, science and good books are all things which will help your mind to grow and be happy; best of all, make sure you take time to read your Bible and good books about it to help you understand it.

The longest Psalm in the Bible (119) is about the greatness and importance of the Word of God. In it, the writer makes some important and challenging statements.

Open Thou mine eyes,
that I may behold wondrous things
out of Thy law.
(verse 18)

O how love I Thy law!
it is my meditation all the day.
(verse 97)

Thy Word is a lamp unto my feet,
and a light unto my path.
(verse 105)

A man who was a great help to me when I first became a Christian wrote this at the front of my first King James Version Bible, 'This book will keep you from sin, or sin will keep you from this book'. That is so true. Do you read God's Word each day?

Female Chaffinch

SUPER SISKINS
– BOLD, BRIGHT AND BEAUTIFUL

Fascinating Facts
An ancient name for the siskin was black-headed goldfinch. They can often be seen in woodland in the company of redpolls. Unlike most garden birds, the siskin has a distinctive forked tail. Their beaks are laterally compressed (squashed from the sides), making them very thin to act like tweezers in extricating seeds from cones.

The little siskin is a bird I usually associate with winter. I remember my first encounter with this pretty little bird on the same holiday as we fed the chaffinches out of our hands.

We were staying in a woodland copse made up of various native tree species. On the first day of the holiday, we purchased a feeder and bag of nuts to see if we could attract anything unusual.

The following day I saw a rather strange-looking finch attacking the nuts with vigour. It was smaller than a sparrow, with feathers a mixture of yellow and green with a black cap. I initially thought it was a small greenfinch but soon discounted that idea. On our next trip to the nearest town, Inverness, I bought an elementary bird book and, scanning through the pages, discovered the siskin.

"That's it," I said to my wife enthusiastically as I pointed to the picture in the book, "it's a siskin that was feeding on the nuts," and so it was.

Male Siskin

Although the siskin is quite common, it is a bird that can be easily missed when a flock are busily fussing around the bird feeders. This summer, a family of siskins visited our bird table every day.

During the second week of that holiday, we took a walk along the banks of the River Findhorn and through a most picturesque valley. At one point, the path joined a small single-track road, and not far along, we spotted a tiny bird obviously in distress on the tarmac. A siskin!

I tenderly picked the small bird up and carefully held it in my hand. It seemed that it was stunned, most probably by a car that had passed along the road. Karen poured a little water into her palm from her water bottle and tried to get the poor fellow (it was a male) to drink. It took several sips and seemed to revive, then as I held my hand out expectantly, waiting for it to fly off, suddenly it flapped its wings a few times, then just keeled over into my open palm – dead!

Once again, that system kicked in when a bird chooses to die rather than live. I held the tiny lifeless body, gently stroking it as if the ministrations of tenderness might bring it back to life. Carefully we made a small hole in the soft woodland earth and sadly buried the unfortunate bird.

For some reason, I have never forgotten that incident, the memory of which floods back each time a siskin crosses my path. It is as if each little finch is saying to me, "I know you tried to help one of us; I have just come to say, 'thank you for caring.'"

I have discovered on my Christian pathway that some Christians are more difficult to get on with than others. Sadly there is the temptation to be uncaring, and we speak and act as if we had never been saved.

The Bible provides some excellent guidance. ***Finally, brethren, whatsoever things are true, whatsoever things are honest, whatsoever things are just, whatsoever things are pure, whatsoever things are lovely, whatsoever things are of good***

Female Siskin

report; if there be any virtue, and if there be any praise, think on these things. ***(Philippians Ch4 v8).***

A great lady missionary to India called Amy Carmichael ran a children's orphanage. She taught the children to ask, 'Is it true, is it kind, is it necessary,' when speaking about others. That was excellent advice that each one of us should try and practice. Just think how many sad and discouraged Christians we could help if each of us just showed a more caring and loving attitude one toward another.

Siskins on feeder

CUNNING CUCKOOS
– THE CLOCKWORK PARASITE

Fascinating Facts
The female cuckoo will lay up to twenty eggs in different bird nests, usually with the same species that reared her. The female will also often eat the egg it replaces in a nest and she can lay a new egg in a new nest every other day. The male cuckoo only sings during the breeding season. Cuckoos love to eat hairy caterpillars that can be poisonous to other birds.

I am sure that we all know what sound a cuckoo makes. It is one of the few birds named after its prominent and distinctive call. The 'cuc-koo, cuc-koo,' sound used to be common during the summers among the trees in the town where I grew up. Seeing one, at least for me, was an entirely different matter.

As a young boy and even into my teenage years, if someone had asked me to describe a cuckoo, I would have been unable to do so. I had no idea; I had never seen one!

Becoming a birdwatcher can be like a policeman trying to solve a crime. Put all the clues together, and you solve the crime, or in our case, unmask the bird!

While walking in Scotland one year, Karen and I often heard the cuckoo's cry, but we had trouble finding the bird. However, we regularly saw an unusual-looking bird of prey resembling a sparrowhawk, but

Cuckoo being fed by Meadow Pipit

something was wrong; it was a strange case! An invisible cuckoo and an unusual hawk!

After looking through the bird guide several times, we put two and two together, realising that what we actually thought was a strange bird of prey was the bird making the cuckoo sound. At first sight of the cuckoo, the mind immediately thinks 'sparrowhawk,' until you have time to realise that not everything the bird is doing ties in with the hawk.

The cuckoo is a parasitic bird. It leaves another bird to raise its young! The female cuckoo will search for a suitable host bird's nest, usually that of a meadow pipit or reed warbler. Once the coast is clear, the cuckoo lays a lone egg in the nest alongside the host's original eggs. The crafty bird can even ensure that the egg markings resemble the other eggs in the nest.

The cuckoo egg hatches before the other eggs, and the first thing the baby cuckoo does is push the other eggs out of the nest, levering them over the side. The baby cuckoo does not want competition in the food stakes from other hatched chicks.

The host parent bird now feeds her 'adopted' young, which develops quickly and soon fills the nest growing much larger than its 'mother' bird.

While all this is taking place, the original parent cuckoo, having laid several eggs in different hosts' nests, is contentedly winging her way south across France, Spain, and into Africa to spend the winter there.

Now, here is another fantastic part of the cuckoo story. When fledged, the young bird finally leaves the care and provision of its host parent and commences on a migration route of thousands of miles south to spend the winter in Africa. The fledgeling embarks on this dangerous challenge without ever knowing its real parents, it has, therefore, never received instruction on what to do or where to fly. This is truly a miracle of creation.

Any sensible discerning person, stopping for a moment and thinking seriously about nature around them, must conclude that behind every human, animal, bird, fish, plant, and tree is the hand of a Creator.

For instance, if the cuckoo had evolved rather than been created, how did the young chick know to tip the other eggs out of the nest? Then how did the young bird learn when to leave, which direction to fly and where to fly? It must have been designed and programmed to act the way it does. Everything about the cuckoo's behaviour points to a 'Creator!'

The more you look around at nature, you can only exclaim, ***'In the beginning God created the Heaven and the earth.'*** ***(Genesis Ch1 v1).***

TERRIFIC TERNS
– ATTACK FROM THE AIR

Little Tern

Fascinating Facts
Terns are some of the world's longest-living birds, often reaching thirty years. Arctic terns migrate (travel) yearly from the Arctic (top of the world) to the Antarctic (bottom of the world) and back, a combined distance of over 20,000 miles. All terns migrate and can only be seen around Britain and Ireland between April and September.

With their long days, the summer months are great for searching the hedgerows and thickets of the seacoast close to home for the various migrating visitors that frequent those places. I especially enjoy scanning the skies about the sea, looking for visiting terns. They are always there with their long black beaks, tipped with yellow – sandwich terns.

Any tern is elegant with its unique slim pointed wings and unusual flapping rhythm. They stand out from the crowd as they dart and swoop low over the waters looking for small fish. Once they sight their prey, they dive into the water to catch it, sit for a few seconds to swallow it, and then take to the air to gain another aerial view of their next meal.

My first fascinating encounter with terns was when I was eighteen and visiting friends in the North East of England for the weekend. On Saturday, we travelled up the Northumberland coast to make the trip across to the Farne Islands. It was here that, many years before, the lighthouse keeper's daughter, Grace Darling, made heroic efforts rowing a boat through a storm to save people from the paddle steamer '*Forfarshire*', which had run aground.

On the day in question, I decided to don a Scottish tartan hat (I love anything Scottish) and a pair of dark sunglasses. We embarked on a small boat to take us to the islands across the short stretch of water. Before we arrived, we were met with the screeches of the nesting arctic terns as they skimmed over the boat at head height as if trying to drive us from their territory. This action gave us magnificent views of their forked tails with long streamer feathers.

Once we had ventured onto the land, the birds attacked with fervent ferocity as they dive-bombed us, seeking to hit us with their feet or, worse, with their razor-sharp orange bills. Was I ever pleased that I had decided to wear the rather daft-looking tartan hat despite the jesting from my friends. It provided excellent protection from the continuous attacks of birds seeking to protect their nests, eggs and young from those they perceived were a danger to their home. Another poor gentleman on the trip with us, who did not enjoy the protection of a tartan hat, received a nasty cut on his head from one of those fearsome beaks.

The experience was never forgotten and is still on my 'must do again' list.

During the summer months, a visit to the pebble beach between Kilcoole and Newcastle in County Wicklow, Ireland, will provide good views of the rare little tern.

This wonderful and active tern, no larger than a blackbird, will thrill watchers by hovering low over the water on fast-beating wings before diving in, hoping to catch a small fish unfortunate enough to be swimming past at the wrong time.

Little terns have a black cap and yellow beak with a black tip almost opposite to the sandwich tern. The sandwich tern, though, is nearly twice the size of the cute little tern.

Sandwich Terns

Thinking of size, consider the caspian tern. This giant among terns grows close to half a metre long. It certainly takes the crown for the largest of the commonly seen terns around Britain and Ireland. You can't help but notice its vast orange bill that leaves all other terns in its wake. All I can say is I'm glad it was arctic terns I went to see on the Farne Islands that day, as my Scottish bonnet would have given no protection from the ferocious bill of a caspian tern!

We all like to feel safe. That is why we use seatbelts in our cars, and many people have an alarm system in their homes. Keeping people safe used to be my job. I would put into place various practices to try and ensure we protected those at work from accidents.

The arctic terns similarly were only protecting themselves and their young when they attacked us. They nest in colonies, all together, to help each other defend themselves and their young. Many animals and birds work similarly, ensuring that together they protect each other from danger around.

God never intended the Christian to 'go it alone' without the help and friendship of others who have also trusted the Lord Jesus as Saviour. This friendship is called fellowship. In Acts chapter 2, the first Christians ***'continued steadfastly in... fellowship.'*** ***(Acts Ch2 v42).*** In other words, they came together regularly to remember the Lord Jesus in what is called the 'breaking of bread'.

They also met collectively to pray and learn together. This time was crucial as it helped them to encourage each other to understand the Word of God and be on the lookout for various dangers. Fellowship with other Christians of different ages is vital – do you enjoy it?

Artic Tern

Superb Small Mammals
– the cute and cuddly

POINTED NOSE SHREWS

Fascinating Facts
Some shrews, including our water shrew, are venomous, and they paralyse their prey by continually biting them, allowing their venom mixed with their saliva to enter the unfortunate victim. Shrews are active night and day, with the female having up to four litters of babies a year, after which she usually dies of exhaustion.

Do you like mice? Some people love them, whilst others hate them, their sudden appearance with their scurrying little feet and long tails making it a frightening experience. I love them; mice, voles and shrews are all little mammals with comparatively long thin tails, which we will link together in this chapter.

It would be a most enlightening project to ask how many readers have seen a shrew. Even though it's the UK and Ireland's most prolific mammal, with over seventy million scurrying around our gardens, fields, parks and hedgerows, I would be astonished if many had come across a living one. They are the secret agents of the animal kingdom, out of sight and undercover!

Not only is the shrew the most abundant mammal it is also the smallest, which is perhaps one reason it stays so well hidden. The pygmy shrew measures no more than six centimetres with a four-centimetre tail, so it is easily overlooked. The common shrew is slightly larger and can grow up to eight centimetres, with a tail from two to four centimetres. Now, it is good to have an idea of size to understand how tiny these creatures are; however, when you see just the slightest glimpse of a long nose as a small furry rodent disappears into the grass, you will hardly be able to tell which shrew it is. The best way to tell them apart is that the pygmy shrew is dark brown, and the common shrew is a lighter brown. Still not an easy thing to gauge in a few seconds of observation.

Shrews are insectivores, meaning they eat insects. They are constantly active on the lookout for something edible, as they need to eat almost their body weight in food daily just to survive. If you are blessed to see a shrew, it will undoubtedly be searching for bugs, grubs, beetles, spiders or some long juicy earthworm.

Shrews are not only smaller than mice or voles; they look different, with a long pointed nose and tiny eyes. I think that their faces look like little hedgehog faces. Look at the photograph and see if you agree. They can also be quite aggressive with each other, sometimes making such a din that humans can hear them fighting in the undergrowth as they pass by.

The life of a shrew is only about one year, but in that year, a female can have three to four litters comprising five to seven babies each. I have read that sometimes the mother shrew will lead the babies around in a train, with each one holding onto the other's tail. I have never seen this behaviour, but I can imagine how incredible it would look.

The closest most people come to spotting a shrew is to find one lying dead on some country path. There is a reason for this. When caught by a predator, the shrew can let off a noxious substance released from special scent glands, making it taste rotten to the hungry creature hoping for a yummy meal. The starving predator will then drop the shrew in disappointment, but sadly, it will usually be dead.

NECKLESS VOLES

Fascinating Facts
Voles are herbivores (plant eaters) and can sometimes kill trees by eating their roots. They will also eat or steal bulbs. The water vole can dive underwater to a depth of 15m. The average life of a vole is six months due to them falling prey to a host of predators such as tawny and barn owls, stoats and weasels.

Naturalists are not supposed to call anything cute; it is just not the done thing. However, I believe that most of the small mammals in this chapter are adorable, and the cutest ones of all are the delightful voles.

You can usually tell a vole and a mouse apart by the head and tail. A vole has a triangular head with no neck; it looks like the head has been stitched onto the body. It also has a much shorter tail than a mouse.

There are three predominant vole species on these islands, the field vole, the bank vole and the water vole. The field vole is the most common, with an estimated seventy-five million. Neither the field vole nor the water vole is present in Ireland. However, the bank vole has been successfully reintroduced recently and is spreading throughout Munster and moving progressively north.

If you are fascinated by all created creatures, you will understand there is the right time to look for wildlife. The commencement of a Gospel meeting, during the singing of the first hymn, was not necessarily the best time to spot something interesting, but that is precisely what happened in one place I was visiting.

I was standing facing the congregation as we sang the opening hymn, when a sudden movement on the carpet to my right caught my attention. I looked in disbelief as a little furry brown creature ran, walked, stopped, and ran again across the carpet. It took a little while to determine whether it was a mouse or vole. The triangular head and short tail confirmed it was a vole, and its darker colour fur told me it was a field vole.

I stopped singing and stood transfixed as the little creature stopped again and looked down the hall in the direction of the people. I had visions of it running towards them, causing mass panic among some of the congregation. It seemed to consider its options for a few moments before scurrying quickly towards a piece of furniture for safety. It darted underneath and out of sight.

I looked around with a smile, wondering if anyone else had spotted the extra visitor to the Gospel meeting. It seemed they hadn't. Then I looked again and noticed a lady grinning broadly. She, too, had seen it but appeared to be the only one. Thankfully there was no mass hysteria or panic, and the little vole decided wisely not to attempt a second showing!

Later that night, when we were back in the comfort and safety of this lady's home, she and her husband told me that this was not the first time a mouse had made an unexpected entrance into the Gospel Hall.

"Well, it just goes to show," I said with a smile, after pointing out that it was a vole that had been in the building, not a mouse, "that maybe the Bible is correct when it tells us to preach the Gospel to every creature!"

MENACING MICE

Fascinating Facts
Most wild mice never live longer than a year. The female house mouse can have up to twelve babies every three weeks! There are four species of mice across the UK and Ireland - wood, house, harvest (smallest) and yellow necked (largest).

Although some people are scared of mice, screaming and jumping on chairs to escape their terrifying approach, watching their little antics can be very captivating. It is always fascinating to discover they have a nest under the shed or a mouse hole or two around the garden, and you never know what else the mice might attract into the garden.

Several years ago, I commenced my five-yearly spring clean of the garage. Jokes have been made, at my expense, that a climbing rope needs to be attached to me to pull me out in case I get lost among the junk! I don't think my garage is quite that bad, but I confess that sometimes it is not far off!

I started moving, sorting, arranging, replacing, and occasionally throwing something out. Then I came to my shelves where I store a multitude of plastic boxes, all filled with odds and ends and bits and bobs that might at some stage come in handy!

I commenced pulling the boxes off the shelves, placing them on the ground, pondering over the contents' usefulness and invariably putting them back pretty much untouched.

Then I saw a cardboard box containing a hanging basket and a bag of compost. It had been in the garage for over a year, so with a sudden flash of gardening inspiration, I thought we should put the basket up somewhere outside the house and fill it with plants.

As I lifted the box down, the bottom right-hand corner was damp and the cardboard soggy. I looked to see if any of my various oils, paints, cleaners, fertilizers, weedkillers or other bottles nearby had leaked. They hadn't.

I opened the top, and an intense aroma hit my nose. It was not unlike the smell of ammonia. As I looked inside, I could see a cluster of little furry bodies packed tightly together, lying sleeping. I had discovered a mouse pad, a genuine mouse pad, a place where mice breed and bring up their young. The potent smell told me these were house mice. What greatly surprised me was that the box was four shelves up, about five feet off the ground. The parent mice must have been budding mountaineers.

I gazed into the box for some time. I was worried that the parents might desert the nest now that I had disturbed their home. What was I to do? It was February and still rather cold outside, especially at night. I decided, therefore, to make life easier for the parents. I left the box on the ground and placed a piece of wood from the garage floor to the top of the box to make a ramp so that the parent mice could get in easier. I just hoped it would work.

I left the light on, closed the garage doors and moved to the far corner to observe. After a rather uncomfortable ten minutes of trying to stand perfectly still and remain noiseless, I saw a mouse gingerly make its way up the ramp and down into the box. I breathed a big sigh of relief.

At lunchtime, I discussed the predicament with Karen.

"You need to put them somewhere outside," she said.

"It's far too cold; the poor little things would freeze," I pointed out.

"But they will destroy stuff in the garage."

"I don't think so; there is nothing for them to eat in there."

"They chew things, anything. You must catch them and put them outside because they will chew anything and make a right mess."

"I'm not putting them outside; that would be cruel," I responded, warming to my role as defender of the mice.

"OK," Karen replied, "but don't tell me I didn't tell you!"

That night as we got ready for bed, I looked outside. The frost was already thick across the garden.

"It's freezing outside," I commented, "I hope the mice are alright."

"I'm sure they will be fine."

"But they might get cold; there is no heating in the garage."

"I suppose you are thinking of putting an electric fire on all night in the garage to keep them warm."

"Yes, I was actually."

Baby mice

"They are mice, and they usually live outside. They will be fine."

"But they might not be. If I put the heater on a timer for fifteen minutes every hour, it would just take the chill off for them."

Karen gave a relenting sigh, knowing she wouldn't persuade me otherwise.

So, I donned my dressing gown, popped on my slippers and headed downstairs to find a timer plug before heading into the bitterly cold night.

I opened the garage door and turned on the light. As I did so, I caught sight of a mouse darting from the box and heading for cover under the shelving units. I lifted a fan heater out of a cupboard, and, having set the timer, I plugged it in and turned it on. I decided that twenty minutes every hour would be better because it was so cold.

When I returned to the warmth of the bedroom, Karen was asleep, and I had no intention of waking her up to inform her of the extra five minutes of heat I was providing.

We left the little family untouched for a week before checking again. When we did, the box and nest were empty. All had survived the dangerous days of dependency upon their parents. They had now left to seek their own homes. I considered my neighbours along the street. Who would be willing to allow a pair of mice to make a home in their garage and offer added heat? I realised that the mice had been very wise by choosing our house and garage. The best thing was that no damage had been done; nothing was chewed or eaten in the garage. I surmised that the little creatures realised they were in a good place, so they knew not to chew what wasn't theirs.

Several months later, I prepared to take a children's meeting in a nearby town. I had purchased a brilliant object lesson sometime earlier to show how sin affects humanity and how the problem can be removed. It comprised three large brightly coloured foam balls, a bar on which they sat, and a cross that could lift one off the bar. The whole contraption had come from America and had been a little costly, significantly the postage charge. It was an impressive visual aid that I enjoyed using.

I placed the box containing the equipment in the car and set off for my meeting. When I arrived, I carried the box in before the children came and opened it up to remove the pieces I required. Sitting in the box were the chewed-up remains of one of the brightly coloured balls used in the presentation; the other two were still in one piece despite having various chew marks here and there. It was clear that mice seemed to prefer purple as that was the ball's colour they had chewed the most! The object lesson was ruined, but, attempting to make the children use a little imagination, I still explained how sin separates and divides us from God and how it can be removed by the work of the Lord Jesus on the cross.

As I drove home that night, I remembered Karen's words, "They chew things, anything, and they will make a right mess." She had been right.

My mother had a saying, 'If you take care of the little things, the big things will take care of themselves.' These tiny rodents, shrews, voles and mice are just little creatures, but they are vital to the rest of creation. Without them, many other birds and mammals would not survive.

An old proverb demonstrates the saying.

For want of a nail, the shoe was lost.
For want of a shoe, the horse was lost.
For want of a horse, the rider was lost.
For want of a rider, the message was lost.
For want of a message, the battle was lost.
For want of a battle, the kingdom was lost.
And all for the want of a horseshoe nail.

If only the nail had been in place, all would have been quite different. The attention to little things in life is the secret to success for every Christian. This may mean doing your best at your school work, helping at home, spending time with someone who is lonely, and I am sure you can think of many more little things you can do well. Being faithful in little things is very important.

And whatsoever ye do, do it heartily, as to the Lord and not unto men; Knowing that of the Lord ye shall receive the reward of the inheritance: for ye serve the Lord Christ.
(Colossians Ch3 v23-24)

MESMERISING HOUSE MARTINS
– ASTONISHING AERIAL ACROBATS

Fascinating Facts
A house martin nest contains around 1000 lumps of mud and clay and can take three weeks to build. One exceptional nest was seen to have eleven house martins living in it. Blue tits and especially wrens will often use vacated nests as winter roosting sites.

I always know when summer is coming when I see some of the first migrating birds appearing around my home. The arrival of the hirundine family, the collective name for sand martins, house martins and swallows, provides a foretaste of approaching summer.

The first to arrive are the sand martins. They excavate their homes in the mud and sandbanks along the beach close to where we live. You can time their arrival almost to the day in mid-March. Next are the swallows and house martins about three weeks later. The swifts are the last to fly in as they noisily chatter on the wing while darting about high up in the sky, looking like small brown boomerangs. The swift, however, is related to the hummingbird rather than the hirundine family.

Incredibly, some of these birds have flown right across the African continent from their winter homes in South Africa. Once they arrive in the British Isles or Ireland for summer, you would expect them to take a rest following such a long and dangerous journey across jungles, swamps, deserts and oceans. Not a bit of it.

Upon arrival, they commence nest building. The sand martins build along some bank overlooking the water. Swallows choose a place inside some open barn, garage or shed, the swifts prefer to nest under roof tiles, and the house martins' location is under the eaves of any other suitable building.

The year we painted the outside of our house, the house martins decided en masse that it was a very desirable residence. When it was concrete grey, house martins attempted to build their domed nest, made from mud pellets, on only a couple of occasions. Once I had completed painting the house white, they saw it in a whole new light!

Day after day, the house martins sought to build their messy, sticky nests under every apex we have – all six. Please don't get me wrong, I love birds and enjoy watching the aerial antics of the house martins; however, their nests make a terrible mess anywhere, especially on the snow-white surface of a freshly painted house!

Out we went with a hosepipe to wash away what they had built before it became too big or they laid eggs in it. As we got rid of one, another apex was chosen as a likely nesting site. While dealing with that new area, others swarmed in, sometimes four at a time, re-commencing work on the space we had just cleaned. It was like the Battle of Britain all over again. House martins, swooping, sticking, arranging, moulding their mud on the wall, trying to complete a suitable nest before we came round again to 'whoosh' it away with a massive water jet.

Eventually, pitting my wits against these aerial wizards, I realised that a plastic 'airball' used by golfers to practice their swings might stop the daily battle. I went up the ladders to drill a small hole in the house wall and attach these little hard balls just where the house martins were attempting to nest. Eventually, with four of the six apexes protected by my super new invention, I stood back to admire my work. This left just the two higher apexes, I could not reach, without protection.

The following day, I checked what the martins were up to, only to discover that they had built a fairly substantial structure right on top of one of my airballs! Then along the wall below another apex, the cheeky little birds placed small mud pellets at strategic intervals, ruining my paintwork!

The battle with them was relentless through May, June, July and August. On one occasion, having rested my ladder against the highest gable to stop them from building, I came out ten minutes later to see a pair of them sitting contentedly upon the top rung. I could hardly believe it. Talk about bold! I felt as though they looked down at me, saying, 'we're the kings of the castle!'

I thought the airball invention would have worked particularly well on top of the alarm box on the rear elevation. No, they just built on top of it, incorporating my airball into their nest!

Finally, in desperation, I decided to place some shiny CDs on the spot they were trying to nest. Often if you put something silvery and shiny up, it deters birds. Karen came up with the idea of foil trays from our barbeque, held off the wall by my little balls. I spent a couple of hours putting them up, and they worked! They really did. The house martins gave up… except on the two high gables that I could not safely reach. At least that made the battle a little easier, with only two places to stop them nesting rather than six!

I was amazed at just how determined these summer visitors were. They never gave up until September arrived, and it was nearly time to fly back across Africa. As they took their winter vacation back to warmer parts, I needed to take out my step ladders and paint again, trying to cover over the mess they had made on my beautiful white walls. What a summer!

I have now purchased a house martin nest box and placed it on the far apex of our garage, just above the barn owl box, which is presently unoccupied. It would be great to have house martins nesting; maybe a family in one area will deter others and keep my walls clean. Time will tell.

It was eye-opening to see how these flying wizards were set on nesting around our house. Their determination was admirable and made me think of the Christian life. Sometimes we find it too easy to give up, throw in the towel and go back to an easier and what may even appear to be a more enjoyable way of life. The Bible, however, tells us that the early Christians ***'continued steadfastly.'* (Acts Ch2 v42).** That means they kept on going, never giving up despite many great discouragements. The book of Hebrews tells us, ***'let us run with patience the race that is set before us, looking unto Jesus.' (Hebrews Ch12 v1-2).***

The words of an old Scottish song seem appropriate.

Keep right on to the end of the road,
Keep right on to the end,
Tho' the way be long, let your heart be strong,
Keep right on round the bend.
Tho' you're tired and weary still journey on,
Till you come to your happy abode,
Where all the love you've been dreaming of
Will be there at the end of the road.

It is important to remember that this world is not our final home; for those who have trusted the Lord Jesus Christ as their Saviour, Heaven is their destination or happy abode, as the poem puts it. When the journey seems hard, it is good to remember that God gives wisdom, knowledge and joy to those who trust Him ***(Ecclesiastes Ch2 v 26).***

The sinner may seem to have many things, but with them often comes heartache and a lack of wisdom and understanding to enjoy them. The apostle Paul wrote at the close of his life:- ***'Notwithstanding the Lord stood with me, and strengthened me... and I was delivered out of the mouth of the lion. And the Lord shall deliver me from every evil work, and will preserve me unto His Heavenly Kingdom: to whom be glory for ever and ever. Amen.*** **(2nd Timothy Ch4 v17-18).**

OUTSTANDING OTTERS
– THE RECLUSIVE FISHERMAN

Fascinating Facts
Otter cubs can be born at any time of the year. An otter's home is called a holt. Wild otters live around five years, but some have been recorded at twice that age. Otter droppings are called 'spraints', these sticky, smelly secretions can often be found on rocks, logs, or other places along a riverbank, providing scent marking to other otters.

I know that otters are not birds, and much of the book has been about birds, but they are mammals and super interesting ones.

I had tried on many occasions and in many locations to see otters. During a trip to the Shetland Isles, a friend, knowing I would love to have the opportunity to watch them, helpfully suggested a well-known otter hotspot that I passed daily on my way to his house.

When I pulled up, it certainly looked the part. A stream was running down to the seashore; rocks, boulders and kelp (a type of seaweed) festooned the area on either side. When the tide was in, everything I could see was covered in the cold waters of the North Atlantic Ocean. Evidently, this was a perfect place to see my first otter.

"Ya just need ta wait a few minutes, ye ken," my friend helpfully informed me, "and yon otters will make an appearance!"

I parked the car, got my binoculars and camera ready and waited… and waited… and waited… and waited! I waited over two hours. Not an otter in sight.

"There are hundreds of 'em around the islands," my friend had promised, "you can't miss 'em!"

I started the car and drove to his house, a little deflated.

"Ya didna see one?" he questioned almost unbelievingly.

"No, I didn't," I replied despondently.

"See 'em every day where you were parked," he enthused.

"Not today," I replied, wondering if I had fallen asleep and missed them, "there was nothing there!"

Several years later, another Scottish island finally produced my first sighting of a real, live, wild otter.

We were on the Isle of Skye and had driven over a narrow, winding road from Breakish to Kylerhea. We had heard that it was not just a beautiful drive, but also there was an otter viewing hide above Kylerhea. It sounded good.

Once we arrived at our destination, having gone over what seemed to me the entire Coolin mountain range, we parked the car.

'Otter hide,' the sign read, 'one mile'.

One mile is not that far to walk for a fit and healthy person. However, I have an aversion to walking needlessly in the rain; it just does not appeal to me in the slightest. It was raining!

Despite my eagerness to see the otters, I was not so eager to get a good drenching in the process.

"Why don't we carry on, get the Glenelg ferry back to the mainland and find somewhere to eat lunch," I suggested helpfully to Karen.

"I thought you wanted to see the otters."

"I did, but not in the pouring rain."

"Well, I would like to see them," Karen replied, getting one of the dogs out of the car.

"And I'm going," our daughter announced determinedly.

So off we trudged, wife, daughter, and dogs striding out ahead and grumpy old me bringing up the rear.

Thankfully it seemed less than a mile to the hide; we went in, appreciating its shelter from the elements.

"Anything doing?" I asked a wizen-faced man sitting staring out to sea through his binoculars.

"I have been here three hours," he replied, "and not one otter!"

My heart sank. I knew that Karen and Grace might, on a good day, stay a maximum of one hour, but the dogs would be bored silly. I'd never see an otter. I had been soaked for nothing!

I became aware of a father at the other side of the hide trying to interest his bored children in the finer points of nature observation.

"What's that over there?" he quizzed.

"Can't see anything but the sea. Sea, sea, sea, is all I can see!" the older boy replied in a monotone voice.

"Can you see an otter?" his father persevered, pointing through the hide window.

"Sea, I can see the sea."

"Can you see anything else?"

"Sky! I can see the sky," the boy responded dramatically.

"Down there, on the shore, among the rocks, that's where to look," his long-suffering father continued.

"Stones!" the boy called out, again in a bland monotone voice; I could see that he was annoying the older couple who had been there for hours. "Stones," he repeated, "I can see the stones. Sea, sky and stones." He was clearly very bored, and the exclamations of the obvious showed his disinterest in being there.

The boy, thinking himself to be quite amusing, tugged his father's sleeve, pointed out the window, and said, "Oh, look!"

"What?" the father asked with somewhat strained patience, following his son's pointing finger upward, "What did you see?"

"More sky!"

Our daughter looked at me as she rolled her eyes, trying to suppress a smile. This latest rather silly outburst from the young lad signalled it was leaving time for the older couple!

"Nothing is happening this morning," the gentleman remarked before lowering his voice and adding, "except for a running commentary. Good luck, I hope you see the otters."

"Thank you," I replied rather dejectedly, hoping I had not got wet on the walk there for nothing.

The three of us took up the seats the couple had vacated in the far left corner of the wooden hide. Here we overlooked an incredible vista of sea, seaweed-covered rocky shoreline and, across the tidal inlet, a heather-clad mountain rising out of the water, bathed in shades of purple. It was a great place to be, even in the rain.

I looked through my binoculars, scanning the shore for any sign of the captivating but elusive otters that we wanted so much to see. I searched for the slightest sign of life, something, anything of interest. Nothing!

I continued to survey the shoreline when suddenly, at the far end of my vision, where a small jetty of stones pushed out into the sea, I saw something moving in the water. A little round head followed by a partly submerged body. An otter!

"There's one!" I said out loud, well within the hearing of the man with the disinterested child.

I pointed to where I had seen it and watched as it scampered out onto the rocks and began eating something it had caught. It was quite a distance away, but we could still see it with the naked eye.

"Look!" said the father, as he pointed the otter out to his two sons who, despite his best efforts, showed no interest in the spectacle before them, "That's what we came to see."

"What?" said the younger boy speaking for the first time.

"An otter," the father calmly responded.

"Can't see it," the older lad replied, "all I can see is sea, and sky, sea and sky, oh and stones!"

I was now beginning to get a little annoyed with the young lad too who seemed to have no interest in the wonderful nature around him. He would probably have been far happier kicking a ball around.

The father threw an exasperated look in our direction, "I think I'd better take them somewhere else," he explained dejectedly, then turning to his two boys, he said, "come on, let's go!"

"Sea and sky, sea and sky, sea and sky and stones," the older boy continued to call out as they left the hide and made their way back along the path towards the car park.

Our daughter, an excellent mimic, could contain herself no more, "Sea and sky," she proclaimed in a relatively good impression of the boy's monotonous voice, "sea and sky and stones!" We all smiled as we thought of the bored child and his poor father's desperate attempts to interest him in the otter. Then we turned our attention back to the shoreline and the antics of this elusive creature.

It had left its perch on the stones and was now swimming through the sea and in our direction. Excitedly, I got my camera out of its case and turned it on, preparing to capture my first wild otter on film. Okay, it's a memory card now, but some of us a little older still remember rolls of film that used to be in cameras.

The otter did not disappoint us as it came out of the water and continued to move along the shore, searching here and there for anything that might be edible - crabs, cockles, molluscs, dead fish.

Otter coming out of the water

It came closer and closer, and I handed my binoculars to my wife and daughter to view it while I clicked away with the camera.

Nearer and nearer, it drew to the shore, directly below the hide. It stopped and looked up as if saying 'hello' to the three of us who were enthralled by its appearance and antics.

"What a pity for that older couple," Karen said, "to have missed this. I wonder if they are still in the car park. I could go and tell them."

"By the time they have made it back here, the otter may have disappeared," I explained.

"I guess you're right."

So, we watched as it dived into the water to swim around a large boulder before returning to the shore. There is no doubt that watching wildlife, God's purposefully designed creatures, is one of the most relaxing and awe-inspiring things anyone can do. It beats wasting time watching TV or playing games on the computer, and even though there are some great nature documentaries, there is nothing quite like seeing nature in real life and observing God's creation with your own eyes.

Finally, the otter disappeared out of sight as it moved further along the shoreline. Its departure was the cue for us to move back to the car and think about lunch. As we left the hide and started back up the track, our daughter mimicked the boy again, "Nothing to see but sea and sky and stones… and otters!"

About three years later, I saw another otter engaging in a most unusual activity during one of my yearly trips to Skibbereen on the extreme south coast of Ireland.

I had decided to take a trip west from Skibbereen towards Mizen Head, Ireland's most southerly point, to look for a pacific diver (a rare seabird), which was residing around Crookhaven.

As I scanned the bay to the west of Crookhaven, I saw the unmistakable form of a grey seal splashing about in the water. It was some way out in the bay. As I tried to hold my binoculars still, I could see it playing with a large stick. It would swim around it, and then seemingly, the stick would somehow move around the seal.

I watched, transfixed at the distant spectacle unfolding before my eyes. It was so entertaining. It was then I realised the stick was no stick at all. It was an otter! The otter and the seal were swimming, splashing and playing contentedly together. Such behaviour was a whole new thing to me. The two mammals were enjoying one another's company.

I grabbed my camera and, trying to hold it steady, attempted to capture some photos of this unique encounter. I was using maximum zoom, which, combined with the constantly rolling water, did not help obtain good pictures of the event. The full zoom can make photos grainy, and the movement of the water makes it quite challenging to focus.

Eventually, after about five minutes, the otter decided it had had enough fun with the seal. It swam to the rocky shore and climbed out. I obtained my best, still grainy image of this remarkable encounter as it scampered up the rocks. The seal, however, stayed in the water with its head in the air looking, I thought rather forlornly, in the direction of its disappearing friend.

I quickly set up my telescope, hoping to obtain better views; however, it seemed that the otter had left his friend and gone in search of other excitement, possibly food, which I am sure it would have no intention of sharing with its seal buddy!

Looking back at the encounter with the boy in the hide is quite funny now. At the time, the boy was bored, embarrassing his father and annoying the other people in the hide. Yet to be able to watch the otter and its antics was fascinating. Sometimes people just look around them and complain when there are some beautiful things to see and be thankful for if only we look carefully. If the boy had wanted to, he could have enjoyed seeing the little otter, swimming and fishing.

There is a little poem that goes like this:

You've got to accentuate the positive
Eliminate the negative
Latch on to the affirmative
Don't mess with Mister In-Between
You've got to spread joy up to the maximum
Bring gloom down to the minimum
Have faith or pandemonium
Liable to walk upon the scene

When you look for the positive, the negative things in life seem very small. If we follow the instructions in the Bible, it tells us *to* ***'rejoice rather, because your names are written in Heaven'*** **(Luke Ch10 v20) and *'rejoice in the Lord always and I again I say rejoice'* (Philippians Ch2 v2).**

Now here is something very interesting and clever. The words 'think' and 'thank' are etymologically related. Wow, what on earth does that mean? Being etymologically related means that both words have the same root or origin. Therefore if we thought more, we would give thanks more. So think carefully, giving thanks to God for your blessings from Him and then you might find a whole lot less about which to complain.

WONDERFUL WOODPECKERS
– THE ORIGINAL ELECTRIC DRILL

Great Spotted Woodpecker

Fascinating Facts
Woodpeckers never wear their beaks out because they are constantly growing, and the continual drilling helps to keep them chisel sharp. They have special feathers that cover their nostrils to stop wood dust and chippings from flying up their noses. There are over 230 species of woodpeckers in the world.

Britain has three species of woodpecker, the great spotted, the most commonly seen, and the sparrow-sized lesser spotted, which occurs in limited places and is never easy to find. Then there is the largest of them all, the green woodpecker with its wonderful green, yellow, white and red cloak of colourful feathers.

When we lived in Yorkshire, England, the local woods were just one hundred metres down our street, and the great spotted woodpecker was a regular and exciting visitor to our garden.

Sadly, where we live now, on the North Antrim Coast of Northern Ireland, there are very few woodpeckers around, and when one is seen, it is put out on social media as a rarity. However, even when they regularly visited the garden, we always had a sense of 'awe' at their arrival. This feeling remains with me today whenever I encounter a 'great spot' as I wander through their woodland home.

If you were to produce some orchestra out of the avian population, then the great spotted woodpecker would have little or no competition at taking its place as the drummer! From January to April, if you walk through woodlands where this wonderfully charismatic bird lives, you will undoubtedly hear it before seeing it as it 'drums' on tree trunks seeking a mate.

The sound it makes, called drumming, is unmistakable, like a quick blast from an electric drill or even the opening of a rusted door as the hinges creak. It is a wonderful resonant noise that, once heard, can not be forgotten. One of the most amazing things is that to create the correct vibrations to produce the 'drumming', the woodpecker must strike the right piece and type of wood up to forty times a second!

To strike wood at such a rate without injuring itself, the great spotted has a unique cushion behind its beak and in front of its brain to act as a shock absorber and protect it from what could be severe brain damage! At one time, engineers seeking to develop head protection for motorcyclists looked closely at this highly absorbent sponge in a woodpecker's head.

The green woodpecker is the comedian as it laughs; the technical word is 'yaffle'. It's a sort of ha-ha-ha-ha-ha…ha…ha. It also drums but not so loudly as the great spotted, and it has a more extended burst with a couple of stuttering beats.

All three varieties of woodpecker feed on insects, although the great spotted is not averse to raiding another bird's nest to steal either its eggs or its young! The beak of the great spotted is designed for hammering into the hardest wood to prepare its home.

The green woodpecker's beak is softer and unable to tackle hardwood jobs. It prefers to peck into soft or rotting wood or even the ground in the hope of finding some tasty grubs or ants for its labours. It is, therefore, much more commonly seen on the ground or, on most occasions, I have encountered it, taking off rapidly from the earth, with its roller coaster up and down flight and distinctive call.

The green woodpecker also has an enormously long tongue that stretches behind its skull that is coated in a particular type of glue. Once the woodpecker has drilled into the wood or earth, the tongue is employed to push into the hole. Here it searches for anything edible that sticks to its surface. The woodpecker then pulls its tongue back into its mouth and enjoys a delicious meal of creepy crawlies, bugs, and other exquisite delights that should be on the McDonald's menu! If you have ever licked out your bowls of jelly and ice cream, you will get the idea.

On one holiday in Norfolk with Karen and her parents, we had just returned to the cottage where we were staying. I looked out of our bedroom window and saw a bird hopping along the edge of the grass at the far end of the large lawned garden. It acted strangely, and I initially thought it was a song thrush looking for snails. Suddenly I realised it was a green woodpecker. I rushed downstairs to grab my camera.

Green woodpeckers are timid birds and take flight easily if they suspect danger. The noise of me bounding around the house looking to find my camera was too much for the bird, and by the time I was ready with the camera in hand, it had disappeared. I ensured, however, that my camera was on the dining table over lunch just in case.

Then a little later, I looked out into the side garden after noticing leaves and soil being thrown around. The woodpecker was back, and this time I was ready. Having foraged in the garden's border for some time, the woodpecker flew onto an old rotting tree stump. I dashed into the sitting room to obtain a better view and took photo after photo as it searched the decaying wood for grubs and bugs. What an exciting lunchtime we had that day.

Undoubtedly the hardest of our three woodpeckers to see is the lesser spotted. The fact that it is no bigger than a sparrow does not help and its preference to remain high up in the tree canopy makes it almost invisible to those searching for it except when the trees are bare. I can pay testament to the lesser spotted's ability to appear invisible as it has eluded all my endeavours to see it!

All woodpeckers have an easily recognised undulating flight, rising and falling up and down as they make their way through the air to land with quite a thud on the trunk of some tree. They certainly are spectacular birds with beaks like pneumatic drills.

The various species of woodpeckers all seem to shout out to us, 'Look, I was created by a great designer!' It couldn't possibly have evolved as some scientists like to tell us. Think just for a moment about those incredible beaks. How would the woodpeckers have ever fed or built a home for the thousands of years they were evolving? What about that tongue? How could the green woodpecker feed itself until it was long and sticky enough? What about that sponge that protects the brain? How did it avoid smashing its brain to a pulp until these protective shock absorbers had fully developed?

Any sensible person has to conclude that there had to be a designer and a creator, ***'For by Him (the Lord Jesus Christ) were all things created, that are in Heaven, and that are in earth, visible and invisible, whether they be thrones, or dominions, or principalities, or powers: all things were created by Him, and for Him.'*** **(Colossians Ch1 v16).**

Green Woodpecker

SENSATIONAL SQUIRRELS
– TREE TOP ACROBATS

Fascinating Facts
A squirrel's home is called a drey and is built high in the trees using hundreds of small sticks, which are weaved together into a round sphere the size of a football. The drey is lined with moss, leaves, strips of tree bark and other soft, warm material the squirrel can find.

As a boy, I used to sit for hours in my bedroom, transfixed by the sight of our resident grey squirrels jumping and swinging through the tree canopy in the garden behind our home. They were absorbing to watch.

We purchased a squirrel feeder at our second home to keep them from eating the birdseed on our bird table. It cost us a good few pounds worth of peanuts to keep it supplied, but it seemed to work to a point. When the feeder was nearly empty, the squirrels would go right inside, allowing the lift-up top that permitted access to close above them. Inside they would chew and munch away contentedly. Sometimes, when seeing this, I would go outside and slowly walk up to the feeder, observing the squirrel through the perspex cover at the front. Inside, it was so engrossed in filling its stomach that it did not see me approaching until I was almost within touching distance. Suddenly perceiving the apparent danger, the top would fly up, followed by the squirrel as it darted like a rocket up the tree to safety.

On a caravan holiday alongside Lake Coniston in the Lake District, we stayed at a campsite known for its red squirrels and as a place frequently visited by green woodpeckers.

The five-mile-long Coniston Water is world-famous as the place where father and son Malcolm and Donald Campbell set numerous water speed records. They used a series of boats named 'Bluebird'. I have never been interested in motor racing, nor have I ever been into fast cars or driving at breakneck speeds. I once won a prize involving a half-day motor racing experience in three different sports cars at a racing circuit called Castle Donnington. As a Christian, I did not need any persuasion that I should not be wasting my time on such frivolities. I phoned up and declined the prize.

However, land and water speed records, that is, driving a car or boat faster than ever attempted before, always interested me as a boy. Whether it was the bravery (or stupidity) of those who undertook, what no one had accomplished before, or the superlative skills of the designers and engineers, or maybe both, I did find such projects fascinating.

Loch Ness in Scotland is famous for its alleged monster; it is also famous for being the stretch of water on which, in September 1952, John Cobb (the first man to drive a car at over 400 miles an hour) took the world's first jet-powered boat 'Crusader'. He hoped to become the first man to break the 200mph barrier on water. He did so too, but tragically as he travelled around 240mph, the boat disintegrated, and the burly, friendly John Cobb died.

In November 1966, Donald Campbell attempted on Coniston to take his boat 'Bluebird' to over 300mph. He had already broken the water speed record on numerous occasions and two years previously had become the only person to ever break both land and water speed records in the same year.

The weather, mechanical issues and funding for the project hampered Campbell. Finally, in the early morning of 4th January 1967, he fired up Bluebird's massive jet engine again and streaked off down the lake, reaching 297mph. He required a little more speed as he returned to set the record. The onlookers watched, and the radio army technicians listened as he returned, providing a running commentary:

"Full power, nose up… pitching a bit down here ... coming through our own wash ... er getting straightened up now on track ... rather closer to Peel Island ... and we're tramping like mad ... and er ... FULL POWER. I can't see much, and the water's very bad indeed ... I'm galloping over the top ... and she's giving a row in here ... I can't see anything ... I've got the bows up ... I'm going ... I'm on my back….U-hh ..."

As he reached 328mph, Bluebird took off, completed a near-perfect summersault and crashed back into the water before cartwheeling along the surface and disappearing in a cloud of spray. Donald Campbell's body was not discovered until 2001!

Each morning of the holiday, I would rise early, creep quietly out of the caravan, and go for a walk, taking time to pray and observe any interesting birds or mammals. As I returned, I often looked over the water's glass-like surface, where the boat and the body at that time still lay, wondering what it would have been like to have been around in 1967 and seen the terrible accident. These men tried to accomplish what they thought were great things, but what a tragic waste of a life given by God. Do make sure that your life isn't wasted trying to accomplish great or dangerous things that bring no true benefit or blessing in your life. The Bible says:

For we are His workmanship, created in Christ Jesus unto good works, which God hath ordained that we should walk in them.

(Ephesians Ch2 v10)

We set up a couple of bird feeders at the caravan, and it wasn't long before our efforts were rewarded with a succession of visiting feathered friends and a couple of red squirrels. I would stand in the awning, camera in hand, and snap away as the squirrels helped themselves to the nuts on offer. When we had them developed, the photos came out very well.

A few months later, the 'Border Fine Art' society ran an 'inspire a figurine competition'. Border Fine Art was a company that created the most beautiful and unique ornaments, mostly of animals or farming scenes. They were quite expensive, so we would try and pick up bits and pieces we liked in shop sales.

They had a collectors club called the Border Fine Arts Society, and one year as a birthday present for Karen, I joined as you received a membership ornament and a glossy magazine four times a year.

Looking at the competition in one of these magazines, I told Karen I could not remember Border Fine Arts producing a model of red squirrels and thought I might send them my photos. I did, they were duly returned with a letter stating that I had won second prize, and a couple of weeks later, an award of a figurine depicting a family of badgers arrived. I confess to being rather chuffed.

A month later, I answered the phone, "Hello, this is Border Fine Arts, Ray Ayres, our senior sculptor, would like to view the photos of the red squirrels again. Would it be possible to send them back?"

I sent them off as requested, and a week later, they were returned with a letter of thanks.

Six months passed, then one day, my mother-in-law, also a Border Fine Art Society member, phoned, "Robert, have you received your copy of the 'Borderer Magazine' from Border Fine Arts yet?"

"No, I haven't".

"Your photos take up two pages; Ray Ayers has created a members-only figurine based on them. It's called 'Autumn Reds'."

I could not wait for the next day's post to arrive. When it did, there were my photos of the squirrels along with a picture of Ray's masterful creation.

It took a few weeks before the sculpture was available for members in the shops. When it was, my mother-in-law phoned again, "They have your ornament in the shop in town". The next time I visited my in-laws, I went to the shop to look.

As I walked in, I could see the glass-fronted display cabinets holding the Border Fine Art range. Almost central was Autumn Reds. I walked up and looked carefully into the cabinet; there were the two squirrels, a fallen feeder, spilt peanuts and a brilliantly detailed tree trunk. The sculptor had, in my opinion, created a beautiful piece of work.

As I contemplated the model, an assistant came and spoke to me.

"Can I help you, sir?"

"No, not really," I replied.

"Beautiful, aren't they, the Border Fine Arts?"

"Yes, indeed. We have a few at home; I came to see Autumn Reds," I explained.

"We only received that last week; it is delightful. Do you know I have a fascinating story about that sculpture."

"Do you?" I responded, surprised.

"Yes, indeed, I do. A lady, a regular customer, came in here earlier this week to order it," she gushed.

It suddenly dawned on me that I might somehow be involved in this story myself.

"Well, this lady told me her son-in-law's photos were used to make this model. Isn't that amazing? And to think she lives locally to here. I believe her son-in-law lives in Yorkshire."

"Yes indeed," I laughed, "I believe he lives in Harrogate."

"Really?" the lady responded, looking like she was thinking hard, "You could be right now, I come to think of it. Do you know this lady then?"

"I should do," I said, grinning like a Cheshire cat, "that lady is my mother-in-law!"

Suddenly the penny dropped, "Oh my, so you must be… I mean… it was your photos… that were used," the poor lady spluttered, "and you live in Harrogate?"

"Correct," I retorted, still smiling.

"Oh my!" the assistant repeated as another customer she obviously knew entered the store; turning to this newcomer, she said, "This man was just telling me that his photos were used to create this ornament."

"It was my mother-in-law who told you," I reminded her.

Eventually, I was able to leave the shop, having enjoyed the feeling of being important. I wondered if that was how the so-called celebrities felt; if so, I thought the feeling must quickly wear off. However, I had enjoyed the fun of the experience just the same.

This incident reminds me of a verse in the book of Hebrews in the Bible.

Let brotherly love continue. Be not forgetful to entertain strangers: for thereby some have entertained angels unawares.
(Hebrews Ch13 v1-2)

As she talked to me, the shopkeeper was unaware that I had any connection with the squirrel figurine or the lady (my mother-in-law) who had visited the shop earlier.

I am certainly no angel or a person of any importance, but I did have some significance to the shop owner for those few moments.

All of us who have trusted the Lord Jesus Christ as Saviour become a saint and, therefore, very important to God. As a result, He expects us to care for one another. The verse from Hebrews reminds us of those in the Old Testament who unknowingly were entertaining angels while offering kindness to strangers. Abraham, Joshua, Gideon and Manoah all had experiences of being visited by angels without initially knowing who they were.

As a newly saved believer, I remember being greatly helped by a couple who practised the truth of Hebrews Ch13 v1-2. They kindly opened their home to me, and I almost lived there at times. I am sure that I must have been a complete nuisance because they already had six children of their own. They showed me how to care for and encourage the Lord's people. I was no angel, but I was entertained richly, not by worldly things, but by a love of the Word of God, His people and His ways.

Autumn Reds made by Border Fine Arts

WINTERING WAXWINGS
– THE SCANDINAVIAN SHOW-OFF

Fascinating Facts
Waxwings breed so that their eggs hatch towards the end of summer, not in the spring. This means plenty of ripe Autumn fruit is available to help feed their young. They roam in flocks, often gorging themselves on berries before sitting quietly for up to thirty minutes to allow their meal to digest.

If you were looking to have a contest for the most colourful birds that visit the United Kingdom and Ireland, the waxwing would come close to the number one spot.

Is it that rather impressive quiff on its head or the black eyestripe? It could be the yellow flash on the wing or the red blot that looks remarkably like old-fashioned sealing wax that gives the bird its name. Whichever it is, the waxwing oozes character!

I first came across them long before the internet or mobile phones existed. I had heard that they were about and rang a number called 'birdline', which cost about ten pence a minute to use in those days. A recorded message gave information about what exciting birds, if any, were about and where. It used to be updated every four or so hours.

I could hardly believe my ears when I phoned it on this occasion to be told that a flock of waxwing were feeding on rowan trees in a housing estate just two miles from our house. I grabbed my camera and headed out at double speed.

They were not easy to miss, and there was plenty of them, as the man on the recording had said 'a flock'. I watched from the car, hardly daring to get out in case they took flight, never to return. As I watched them flit between branches gorging themselves on the bountiful supply of rowan berries the trees offered, I remember thinking that I had never seen such a stunning bird.

After sitting in the car watching and admiring them for about fifteen minutes, I cautiously ventured out, observing that they seemed oblivious to a man walking past with his dog.

I approached, camera in hand and ready, hoping to obtain some great shots of these rare and majestic visitors to our country. In those long-gone days of cameras having rolls of film, I knew I needed to be cautious in the number of photos I took. A roll of film holding thirty-six prints cost around five pounds to develop, so, unlike today's digital memory cards, taking a multiplicity of images could be expensive.

I focused on one bird sitting closer to me than most and pressed the shutter. Having taken several of what I hoped would be good pictures, I realised I was no longer alone on the pavement. I had been joined by a little old lady who seemed to be having difficulty deciding what to look at, me or the waxwings!

"How tall are you, young man," she enquired in a friendly way.

"Young man," I repeated, "I like that!"

"Like what?" the lady questioned.

"That you called me a young man," I replied, "I like it."

"Well, you are compared to me."

As I looked more closely at her wrinkled face, bent frame and walking stick, I realised that perhaps the initial complement wasn't all I took it to be.

"Anyway," she continued, "I'm more interested in your height than your age. You're tall."

"I know", I agreed, "I'm six feet five and a half inches."

"Well I never," the old lady responded, "I thought you were taller than that. Seven feet, I'd have said!"

"No, no, not that tall," I assured her, "Half an inch short of a giant."

"A giant! Well I never. Don't suppose there are too many giants in the world if you have to be seven feet and half an inch to be one."

"No," I explained, "I'm half an inch short. A giant is officially six feet six inches – two metres."

"Well, I never, is it by gum? You learn something new every day."

"Yes. There is a giant's club, but I'm half an inch short to get in."

"Well I never. Try standing on tiptoes!"

"Pardon."

"Stand on tiptoes, and you'll get in."

"Get in where?"

"The giants' club!"

"Oh, I see. I'm afraid you need to be measured officially."

"Well I never!.... Watching them parrots, are you?"

"What?" I questioned, looking at the lady in puzzlement.

"The parrots, been there a couple of days they have. Don't know where so many escaped from."

"Waxwings!" I corrected her, explaining why I was on the pavement.

"What did you say?"

"The birds are waxwings."

"Never knew there was any other name for a parrot. A parrot is a parrot as far as I ever knew."

"These are not parrots."

"They aren't?"

"No, they are waxwings. They have come from Scandinavia."

"My neighbour told me they must be escaped parrots."

"Well, your neighbour was wrong. These are waxwings. They occasionally arrive here in winter when their food supply runs short in Norway, Sweden and Denmark."

"Well I never. So they are not escaped parrots?"

"Certainly not, these are wild birds."

"Oh, they aren't parrots," the lady replied as if trying to convince herself that the exotic birds that had taken up residence in her street were not parrots,"what do they eat?"

At this point, I felt like answering, roast beef and Yorkshire pudding, as we stood together watching the flock devour the rowan berries like there was no tomorrow.

Instead, I answered politely, "Rowan berries, those are rowan trees."

"Well, I never. What do you call them again?"

"Rowan berries," I answered helpfully.

"The birds, not the berries!"

"Waxwings."

"I will tell my neighbour right away, and they come from Sardinia?"

"Scandinavia," I repeated, "Norway direction."

"Well, I never."

The dear old lady shuffled off down the street to relate her newfound discovery to her neighbour.

I have often wondered if she ever remembered their name, or did she call them 'boxwings,' or 'foxwings', or 'lapwings,' or maybe she just stuck with parrots!

The photos I took that day came out very well, and I was delighted to have seen this rare visitor for the first time.

It was another twenty years until I had the pleasure of coming across them again. This time it was ten miles from our home in Northern Ireland.

A small flock of about fifteen birds stayed high up in the canopy of some tall pine trees close to the main road. Several rowan trees were alongside the slip road, which provided sustenance for these long-distance flyers.

I visited the flock several times, as their visit was around the Christmas holidays. Several people stopped their cars to ask what I was doing, gazing into the sky through either my binoculars or my camera — some asking to borrow my binoculars to have a closer look.

Although I spoke to quite a few visitors where the waxwings stayed, I never did have such an interesting conversation as I had done with the dear old lady so many years before. It proved to be a very memorable day!

Waxwings are very showy birds, and it almost seems they are shouting out for attention in one way or another. Once you see them, you cannot help but keep looking at them; they are so captivating, and they can eat! Some people have counted them eating between five hundred and a thousand berries over six hours. Despite my interest in all things feathered, I confess that I would not have the patience to undertake such a survey, impressive though the findings were.

The waxwing is a confident showy bird, and with its good looks, it definitely does have something to be proud about. When the Lord Jesus came to this world, it was not to be admired or to draw attention to Himself, and He often retreated away from the crowds. Instead, the Lord Jesus came to show us the way of salvation, to minister to the needs of others and to die on a cross for our sins.

As Christians, we should be different in every way from people of the world. We should not want to show off or be the centre of attention. We should strive to let others see Christ in and living through us. The Bible states, ***'that in all things He might have the preeminence'*** ***(Colossians Ch1 v18).*** This verse means that the Lord Jesus should have the central place in our lives. This is a challenge to us all. Do you like people to be captivated with you, your talents and abilities, or do you prefer to show the character of your Saviour?

SURPRISING SPARROWS
– CHEERFUL, CHEEKY AND CHIRPY

House Sparrow

Fascinating Facts
Most pairs of house sparrows will have two broods of chicks a year, and those who start breeding early may manage to have three. The male and female tree sparrow look alike and usually remain faithful to each other for life.

When I visit schools giving my 'bird talks', I always speak of the size of birds, comparing them to two that I presume most children are familiar with, the blackbird and the sparrow. I have however, discovered that many children have little idea of what a common sparrow is, never mind what size it might be, hopefully after this chapter you will all know a lot more.

To anyone without any genuine interest in birds, the sparrow might come under the term 'LBJ' – 'little brown job', especially the female. LBJ is a term used among birdwatchers (collectively called 'birders') for any bird that is difficult to identify at first sight, usually because its primary colouring is brown. Such birds as garden warbler, dunnock and corn bunting come to my mind when I think of LBJs.

The sparrow is a beautiful little bird when you carefully study it. We are fortunate to have both sparrow species visiting our bird table daily in the garden. The more common house sparrow is wonderfully marked.

The male has a grey crown leading to a brown area around his head which stretches down to the back where its wings are a delightful mottled hue of browns, greys and blacks. It also has a uniform light grey from its cheek to its tummy.

Then there is the 'bib,' an area from below its beak to its chest that is black. This black area reminds me of an ink stain that started small and narrow and spread over its chest. This colouring of its 'bib' is significant for sparrows, as the larger it is, the more dominant the bird. A sparrow with a sizeable black chest might well be 'lord of the manor', whereas a sparrow with a smaller 'bib' or one that is not so boldly coloured could be subservient to the bigger, brighter, bolder bird. It also makes a massive difference when it comes to mating.

A sparrow with a more prominent bib will always have the first pick of the available females. These female sparrows will want the male's genes to feed through to their own young, so such a male will always be in demand.

House sparrows have a sad past of persecution through the years; millions have been captured and killed because they were considered in the same league as rats - vermin!

Sparrow clubs were formed not to protect the birds but to capture and kill them, with church clergy often paying a monetary reward for every dead bird. Sparrows were regularly eaten for their meat, such as it is, and 'sparrow pie' was a regularly enjoyed meal. Sadly, many ways were created to catch and kill the birds, including scaring them out of their nesting places; then, as they flew out in alarm, a group of young people would be waiting with something like tennis rackets in hand to swat the unfortunate birds out of the sky. Thankfully times have changed, and these busy little birds are protected by law from further persecution.

The other species of sparrow is the tree sparrow. This bird is slightly smaller than the house sparrow, with a most striking chestnut crown and black cheek marking as if someone has added a dab of black paint.

The bib is also considerably smaller in the tree sparrow, rarely dropping below its neck and usually more triangular. Then around the neck is a beautiful white circle that reminds me of a vicar's collar.

It took me years to see my first tree sparrow, as they are not that common in Britain and Ireland. However, a trip to China and some of its close Asian neighbours would show that in those countries, the tree sparrow is just as numerous as their more common cousin, the house sparrow. Over the years in those countries, the tree sparrow suffered similar persecutions as those inflicted upon our house sparrows.

Many ornithologists devote much time searching for birds they have not seen. In my case, I look while out walking or on holiday. So, on one of our holidays to Scotland, we decided to visit a place just off the A9 near Aviemore called 'Landmark Forest Adventure Park'. It was a great place to take a ten-year-old daughter as there were water slides, a woodland boardwalk in the tree canopy called the 'Red Squirrel Nature Trail', a shop and a host of other seemingly exciting activities. I was delighted to discover too, that it was an excellent place to see Scotland's famous crested tit, a little bird I have always wanted to see but that only lives in a specific part of the Scottish Highlands. Here then, was my opportunity.

Having negotiated the treetop nature trail, we stopped at a wildlife feeding area. A red squirrel was undoubtedly making the most of a bountiful supply of nuts in its unique squirrel feeder. All three of us stood for quite some time, watching this gorgeous little creature eating its way through a collection of nuts.

I kept an eye out for my crested tit, 'That would make the day,' I thought as I watched the chaffinches, blue tits, great tit, coal tits, greenfinches, and the occasional siskin fly onto the feeders to enjoy the available food.

Suddenly a more unusual bird caught my eye. It was a sparrow, but not a 'normal' sparrow. It was different, smaller, brighter with the unmistakable 'vicar's collar'. My first tree sparrow. I was so excited, and as I pointed it out to my wife and daughter, I am sure others nearby wondered why a grown man could become so animated about a sparrow.

Now I see them daily and having them nest in my garden, I do not fully appreciate them as I perhaps should. They are still engaging, fluttering onto the bird table and diving deep into the nearby hedge at the first sign of danger. Seeing them regularly, even though they are not particularly common around the United Kingdom, I have lost the thrill I had on that first occasion I sighted these great little birds.

I am so glad that the sparrow is mentioned in the Bible when other, more popular birds such as the robin are not. It lets me know that God cares for all, not just the clever, special or privileged, but everyone. A verse that everyone should know well tells us this:

Tree Sparrow

Male House Sparrow feeding young

'For God so loved the world, that He gave His only begotten Son, that whosoever believeth in Him should not perish, but have everlasting life.'
(John Ch3 v16)

Whoever you are and whatever your background is, you are loved by God! The Lord Jesus used an example about sparrows to show this.

Are not five sparrows sold for two farthings,
and not one of them is forgotten before God?
But even the very hairs of your head are all numbered.
Fear not therefore: ye are of more value than many sparrows.
(Luke Ch12 vs 6-7)

If God cares for all the sparrows in the world, He certainly cares for you! He cared enough to send His Son to die on a cross to pay the price for your sin. Are you concerned enough about your soul to turn from your sin, trust the Lord Jesus and start for Heaven?

POWERFUL PEREGRINES
– THE BIRD THAT HELPED WIN THE WAR

Fascinating Facts
Peregrine's usually mate for life and return to the same nest site each year. One peregrine ringed and recorded in 1992 was found again in 2012, making it over twenty years old. In Tudor times, the peregrine was given protection by royal decree, making it one of the first birds to become a protected species.

Sometimes we believe that we have to go to some exotic place to see all the best wildlife; giraffes, elephants and lions in Africa; tigers in India; Kangaroos and Koalas in Australia and bears in Canada. This, however, is not always the case as there can be some pretty extraordinary wildlife very close at hand.

Imagine seeing a bird that is the fastest known creature in the world. It can dive onto its victims at around two hundred miles an hour. Think about seeing a wild bird that helped shape the course of the Battle of Britain and, ultimately, the Second World War. Please meet the peregrine falcon.

I well remember the first time I knowingly saw this incredible bird. I was walking the North Coast cliff path on the island of Jersey when I looked towards a rock below me to see a bird sitting there, gazing back at me. It was about a hundred metres away and close enough to see with the naked eye and make out that it was a peregrine falcon. The large black eyes, the grey head with grey sideburns running either side onto its cheeks and the grey and white mottled breast make this bird unmistakable. I could hardly believe my eyes as I tried to carefully lift my camera from its case and take off a few pictures before it flew away. What a thrilling bird to see!

Unfortunately, I forgot to make a mental note about where I had seen it on the cliff path. Raptors (the collective name for birds of prey) often have favourite perches to which they repeatedly return. About ten years later, walking the same path, I recognised the very rock upon which the peregrine had been sitting. This time the rock was occupied by a kestrel – but that's another story.

Having found the rock again, I was delighted to discover it was just two hundred metres from a remote car park. Its location made regular visits reasonably straightforward. To find out what else used this popular spot as an observation post, I returned to it daily during my stay on the island, and not just to look for more peregrines or kestrels. The dense foliage on either side of the path to the rock was alive with birdlife, linnets, wrens, chiffchaff and the superb cetti's warbler.

It took a few days (by which time I was becoming a little frustrated) to see a peregrine once again. It was a Wednesday evening, and after enjoying tea at the house of friends, I decided to try once more.

The island of Jersey is only forty-five square miles in size. It runs roughly nine miles east to west and five miles north to south. Many living on the island consider driving from one side to another akin to going on holiday. It just isn't done! I remember a local person being amazed that we had visited two garden centres six miles apart on the same day!

I set off the five-mile drive as the sun started to sink in the west. The sky was a beautiful russet red, and the shadows were beginning to lengthen rapidly when I pulled up in the car park from which I could walk to the 'rock'. As soon as I started along the path, I could see that something was in residence. Even from two hundred metres away its grey appearance made me sure it was the long-awaited peregrine. A quick scan with my binoculars confirmed the initial observation.

I pulled my camera out of its bag, set it up and began to take photos. The marvellous sixty times optical zoom lens certainly helped; I was still too far away, though, to obtain perfect images. However, I wanted something to record the moment if it flew off.

Carefully and slowly, I made my way along the path all the time, fearful that someone coming the other way talking too loudly or taking their doggy friend on its evening walk might disturb the peregrine and cause it to take flight. I edged closer, down to one hundred and fifty metres, then one hundred. I could hardly believe it as I finally stood still, looking at this most impressive predator from less than fifty metres. The bird took on a slight yellow hue reflected off the sky as the shadows and colours caused the automatic focus on my camera no end of bother.

Eventually, I lifted my binoculars and contented myself, admiring the streamlined shape, the wonderfully mottled breast and big dark eyes that can pick out its prey from a two-mile distance — what a bird.

Then it was gone. Off and away round the small headland and out of sight. How glad I was that, on a whim, I had decided to head back to the cliffs once again.

Raptors (birds of prey) are at the top of the list of 'apex' hunters. These are birds that take other birds and mammals for food. Amazingly the peregrine, given half a chance, is happy to add other raptors such as kestrels and even owls to its diet.

During the early days of World War Two, the Royal Air Force was having a hard time defending the British Isles from the might of the German airforce, the Luftwaffe. Throughout 1940 German bombers regularly attacked major cities causing catastrophic damage, thousands of deaths and unimaginable suffering.

British Hurricane's and Spitfires defended the islands in what history has recorded as the Battle of Britain. One innovation the pilots made was to fly high with the sun behind them. The sun's brightness hid the aircraft from the view of the attacking Luftwaffe formations until the British planes were diving down upon the surprised Germans.

The British fighter pilots had learnt this strategy from watching the peregrine falcon's hunting technique of diving upon its victim out of the sun. By copying this behaviour, the Royal Airforce won this vital battle that ultimately led in part to the final victory that would occur five years later.

I have seen peregrines many times since those encounters in Jersey. They are often around the cliff paths near our home. I still marvel that any creature can reach a speed of two hundred miles an hour. I consider it an honour anytime this incredible bird stays long enough for me to enjoy its presence.

Two hundred miles an hour is well over three miles a minute. That is pretty fast! Did you know that you might travel much quicker than that one day if you are saved? Faster than a plane or rocket! How?

The Lord Jesus left a promise, ***'And if I go and prepare a place for you, I will come again, and receive you unto Myself; that where I am, there ye may be also.' (John Ch14 v3).*** The Lord Jesus is coming again for His people, who have trusted Him as Saviour. When that occurs, Christians will be taken straight to Heaven without dying or suffering; however, those left behind will have missed the opportunity to be saved and will never be in Heaven.

How quickly will this happen? The Bible says, ***'In a moment, in the twinkling of an eye, at the last trump: for the trumpet shall sound, and the dead shall be raised incorruptible, and we shall be changed.' (1st Corinthians Ch15 v52).*** This remarkable change will occur so fast, much faster than an eye blinks, so we must be prepared before it happens. Are you ready?

STUNNING STONECHATS
– VIBRANT AND VIVACIOUS

Male Stonechat

Fascinating Facts
Between 50,000 and 60,000 pairs of stonechats live in the UK and Ireland. During courtship, the male stonechat will often hover, passing over the female up to twenty times while she sits on the ground fluttering her wings to encourage him.

As a boy of around eight, I remember learning of a true story called 'Born Free'. It was about the raising and reintroducing to the wild of a lion cub called 'Elsa'. From that moment, I was interested in wildlife.

After hearing the story, I surveyed our garden, wondering how to get more wildlife to visit. I knew that lions, giraffes, antelopes and elephants in the story were highly unlikely to visit the garden of a semi-detached house in suburban Harrogate! I did consider how I might attract more birds and incorporated one or two not-so-successful innovations to encourage them.

Sadly at school, in my day, and maybe more so today, it was not 'cool' to be into wildlife, and I remember being laughed at for knowing what a pied wagtail was.

Over time, other pursuits squeezed out the desire for all things furry or feathery; exams, college, work, and marriage.

Then, a holiday in Devon, just before our daughter was born, rekindled my interest in feathered creatures.

During this holiday, we enjoyed daily walks around Devon's cliff paths and beaches. Occasionally an interesting looking little bird flittered around us that kept me wondering what it was.

However, it happened on our way back to our accommodation travelling along a narrow country lane. As we drove on a relatively straight part of the road, I suddenly spotted an almost tropical-looking little bird sitting on a fencepost.

I anchored on the breaks, saying to Karen, "What was that?"

"What was what?"

"That bird!"

"What bird?"

Female Stonechat

"Something I have never seen before. It was beautiful."

I reversed the car back along the lane, half expecting the little thing to fly away at the suspected danger my car might present. It did not. It stayed put.

"Oh, wow!" Karen said, spotting the bird for the first time, "What is it?"

"No idea," I replied, transfixed by the black head, white collar and incredibly orange breast of this fantastically coloured little creature.

We both sat in the car, captivated by the stunning colour and pose until the 'toot toot' of another vehicle that had stopped behind us caused the bird to fly away and hinted that it was time for us to move on.

"I've never seen one of those before," I commented.

"Me neither."

The next day we headed into Barnstable to purchase a bird guide. Thumbing through the pictures of this introductory guide, we soon found a bird called 'stonechat'.

"That's what it was," I exclaimed delightedly at my discovery, "a stonechat!"

I flicked excitedly through the book's pages rediscovering the birds I had enjoyed watching as a child. I was fascinated as I looked at pictures of skylarks, meadow pipits, and other countryside birds I had grown up with while staying at my parent's caravan on Yorkshire's east coast.

As we walked daily, bird guide in hand, we took special note of every bird, eagerly looking through the guide to identify those we did not know.

Then we saw again the unmistakable black head, white collar and orange chest — another stonechat.

In Northern Ireland, throughout the summer months, we see the stonechat regularly as we walk our dogs along the coastal paths near our home. To my family's chagrin, I am still compelled to take a photo of the stonechat every time I see it. I have a more extensive collection of pictures of this colourful little bird than any other. It is a bird that loves to sit up and show off on top of posts, bushes and trees. It is a photographer's delight while making its easily recognisable 'chat, chat' call.

I'm very thankful that this bright, noisy little bird rekindled within me a love for all things furry, fluffy or feathered.

The Christian life can be similar to my experience with wildlife. It can become so easy to get out of touch with God. Life seemingly becomes too busy with so many things pressing in on our time; even an interest in wildlife can become a hindrance if it keeps you from

Male Stonechat

the things of God! King David in the Old Testament had just such an experience. He had allowed sin to come into his life and ruin his relationship with God. When he confessed this, he asked, ***'Restore unto me the joy of Thy salvation'*** **(Psalm 51 v12).**

Thankfully when Christians fail and fall, God is always willing to forgive us, help us and use us again. Our peace with God is restored on confession of our sin to Him. The cheery little stonechat rekindled my enthusiasm for birds. It may be that if your love for the Lord and interest in His things have grown cold, the Lord will bring something across your path to make you stop and think. If anything in your life comes between you and God, the best thing to do is leave it and keep your relationship with God as your number one priority. ***'See that you refuse not Him that speaketh.'*** ***(Hebrews Ch12 v25).***

Juvenile Stonechat

CRAFTY KESTRELS
– THE AVIAN HELICOPTER

Fascinating Facts
During winter, kestrels prefer to hunt by perching and looking for prey as it uses less energy than hovering. The country name for a kestrel is 'windhover', which describes the bird's features and its use of the wind to keep it airborne, adjusting its wings and tail to catch headwinds and updraughts while keeping its head perfectly still.

As you travel motorways and dual carriageways, you will often encounter a kestrel hovering over the grass verge, watching the ground intently below for signs of its next meal. Kestrels are seen so frequently hovering like this that they are often nicknamed 'motorway hawks'.

When you become interested in birds, you soon discover that birds are placed in families. For example, the thrush family includes, unsurprisingly, song thrush and mistle thrush. However, blackbirds and our winter visitors, redwings and fieldfares also belong to this family.

Raptors (birds of prey) are just the same but it is perhaps a little more challenging to place them in families of hawks, falcons, harriers, kites, eagles and owls, to name a few. The kestrel is a falcon, not a hawk, so technically, the term 'motorway hawk' is incorrect. Sadly, there is no easy way to learn which bird of prey belongs in which family.

My, not so simple method runs like this:-

- **Falcons fall fast** – peregrines and kestrels fall on their victims and have pointed wings for speed.
- **Hawks walk** – these tend to be slower in flight – although this is not always noticeable when, for example, a sparrowhawk makes a bee line for the bird table. They have shorter, more rounded wings.
- **Harriers hunt** - flying low and deliberately over fields looking for mice and voles.
- **Owls are night owls** – usually seen at night.
- **Osprey spray** – they are water birds that dive into lakes to catch fish, causing a spray as they hit the water.
- **Buzzards are bold** – they sit in the open on fences or telegraph poles.
- **Eagles** – are just so big as to be obviously nothing else than an Eagle.

The kestrel's ability to hover is unique among birds in Britain and Ireland. Although other birds, such as buzzards and some terns, can perform this extraordinary feat, none can match the skill of the kestrel. The buzzard will only hover occasionally and is certainly not the master of stationary flight like the kestrel.

Whenever I see the kestrel, I think how incredible it is to remain stationary in the air using its wings and tail feathers to maintain its position. Then I think of the poor tiny shrew, mouse or vole, unaware of the fatal danger above them.

At the time of my first sightings, I did not know that the kestrel also possesses another remarkable feature, perhaps even more incredible than its ability to hover; it has a kind of infrared eyesight.

As a boy, I thought the kestrel was hovering, looking for the movement that would give away the presence of some poor little mammal it was hoping to catch for its lunch. How wrong I was! It was using its remarkable eyesight to look for – wait for it – urine! Yes, that's correct. It was watching for when its perspective prey went to the toilet! When it sees the heat from the mammal's urine, it traces it back to its source, dives and pounces on the poor unsuspecting creature. Ingenious or what?

On one occasion, when I was in Jersey, I kept a close eye on a rock I knew raptors used as a lookout perch. The same one is mentioned in the chapter on peregrines. After taking photographs of wrens bringing nesting material to a nest site, I saw a kestrel land on the rock. What was so exciting was that it had something in its talons, I lifted the camera and began to click away as I steadily drew nearer to the murder scene. Unlike a human criminal, the guilty party seemed unphased by my presence as it tore into the mouse it had caught. Holding its catch tight, it picked off pieces with its razor-sharp beak as I carried on snapping away. I knew this was something rather special that I had to capture on my camera.

After about five minutes, the kestrel became bored with taking small bites. Therefore, it picked up the rear end of the unfortunate mouse and began to swallow it whole as if it wanted to show me how very clever it was. I watched, transfixed, as the dead creature rapidly disappeared into the falcon.

Once the meal was over, the kestrel remained sitting contentedly upon its perch as if savouring every moment of the lunch it had just gulped down. After ten minutes, the bird decided it was time to fly away and leave me alone. The problem was it was so full it could hardly lift off!

It took to the air but landed about twenty-five metres further along the path I was standing on. I closed in for another few pictures with my camera. However, believing it had given me enough of its time, it took off again but only managed ten metres before returning to the path. As I drew nearer, it flew up and out about twenty metres into the ferns, where it landed and disappeared among the foliage. It was no doubt hoping that out of sight among the vegetation, I would not disturb it again. I didn't, as I had no desire to negotiate a steep embankment with a cliff below. I left the bird to enjoy digesting its catch.

It's fascinating watching a kestrel hunting all day, hovering, moving a few metres, hovering, changing position, patiently hovering again, then suddenly diving in a controlled descent towards some unsuspecting rodent. As a young boy, I remember trying to follow them as they hunted over the fields around my parent's caravan. The colours, especially the male, are striking and the most vivid of all the resident raptors across Britain and Ireland. The grey head, tear-stained cheeks, russet brown body and yellow legs and feet make the kestrel a rather impressive-looking bird. I have, on a few occasions, watched a buzzard hovering. They can do it, but not for as long, and their wide wingspan and large bodies make them look ungainly compared to the effortless control of the kestrel.

As any reader of this book should be aware, reading the Bible daily is imperative for any Christian. The Bible is not just a textbook full of instructions, guidance and commands to be remembered and obeyed. No, it is a book of wonderful promises from God. I have recently tried to think of a Bible passage I can recall when I see a particular bird. I have not got too far; however, here are a few.

Eagle – a promise from God:

But they that wait upon the Lord shall renew their strength; they shall mount up with wings as eagles; they shall run, and not be weary; and they shall walk, and not faint.

(Isaiah Ch40 v31)

Sparrow – the Lord Jesus dying alone on the cross for our sins:

I watch, and am as a sparrow alone upon the house top.

(Psalm 102 v7)

Robin – the red breast reminds us of His blood:

The blood of Jesus Christ His Son cleanseth us from all sin.

(1 John Ch1 v7)

Blackbird – a beautiful singer:

Let the Word of Christ dwell in you richly in all wisdom; teaching and admonishing one another in psalms and hymns and spiritual songs, singing with grace in your hearts to the Lord.

(Colossians Ch3 v16)

I am sure you will be able to think up far more. Try and find a link between the bird and the Bible. Then when you see the bird, you can remind yourself of the Bible passage.

When it comes to the kestrel, my mind goes to the Psalms and the beginning of Psalm 91:

He shall cover thee with His feathers, and under His wings shalt thou trust: His truth shall be thy shield and buckler.
(Psalm 91 v4)

God is a God of love, mercy and compassion, which, sadly, many forget. Instead of desiring to swoop down and kill, like the kestrel, God wants to save, shelter and shield all who have trusted His Son as Saviour. God reveals Himself as a great bird hovering over us and protecting us from the danger around us. This is a promise to enjoy!

Kestrel eating mouse

NEAT NUTHATCHES AND TANTALISING TREECREEPERS – THE YO-YO BIRDS

Treecreeper

Fascinating Facts
Nuthatches never travel far from home, often staying within a mile radius of their nest site. Nuthatches are absent from Ireland. The nuthatch is the only bird in Britain that walks down a tree trunk headfirst.

Treecreepers will often join flocks of tits, especially in winter, as they scour woodland looking for food. Like the nuthatch, they never move far from their place of birth. Treecreepers press their sturdy tail feathers against the bark of a tree to provide extra stability as they climb.

If you are ever walking through woodlands, nuthatches and treecreepers are the two birds to enjoy finding.

The treecreeper moves almost mouse-like up the trunk of a tree, its curved beak checking out every nook and cranny for a tasty spider or juicy grub. It will land near the base of the trunk and commence scurrying up and around the bough. They choose trees with particularly rough bark, such as oak and scot's pine, as this surface type will hold significantly more insects hidden away.

You will notice if you see one that the treecreeper never comes down a tree trunk headfirst; it only ever goes up.

In Northamptonshire in England, there is a small private nature reserve. When visiting the area, I decided to visit the reserve to obtain some photos of less familiar birds for use in my nature talks in local schools. Entering one of the hides, I met a younger man with the most sophisticated camera and lenses I believe I have ever seen. It was huge. 'This man must be not just an expert ornithologist but also a professional photographer,' I thought as I looked rather enviously at his equipment.

"Much about?" I questioned as I took a seat and commenced scanning the area in front of the hide.

"Just a few birds here," he replied, motioning with his camera towards a well-stocked bird table visited by a couple of chaffinches.

Anyone keen on birding will know we call birds by their names, never saying, 'just a few birds here'. I suspected that he was maybe not a professional after all.

"I take it your into wildlife photography?" I quizzed, pulling out my own comparatively speaking, highly inadequate bridge camera.

"No, not really," he replied amicably, "I'm more into landscapes and buildings. I live in Milton Keynes; it's a bit short on good landscapes, so I thought I'd try taking some bird photos."

"Excellent," I responded enthusiastically, "although birds are maybe not as accommodating as landscapes for taking photos."

"No, they aren't," he laughed, "you have to be quick."

"Has anything interesting visited the table so far?"

"Just those pink and grey birds," he offered, pointing to a chaffinch, "and are those blue tits?"

They were. My new companion may have been a wiz with a camera, but he knew little about his subject matter.

I had just settled into position, looking out of the hide, across a small pond with overhanging branches, when movement caught my eye. Redpolls!

I snapped a few quick photos before informing the man with the camera, "There are a couple of redpolls up here."

"Red poles?" he questioned suspiciously.

"Yes, they are a small finch. A type of bird," I added hastily, just in case he thought I was trying to point out to him two poles in the distance painted red!

"Got them," he exclaimed, pointing his camera in their general direction.

"They tend to live in Scandinavian countries," I enthused, "and they build a wonderful three-layered nest of twigs, moss and feathers."

"Never heard of them," he replied, snapping away, "thanks for pointing them out."

"No problem. Have you seen the siskins?"

"What skin?"

"Siskins, over there. See those two hanging upside down trying to get the alder seeds."

"Those little green and black birds?"

"That's them."

"Wow, never heard of them either," he responded, repositioning his camera to obtain a better angle from which to photograph them.

"What do you call them? Red skins?"

"No, those are siskins, and the little red, grey and brown birds are redpolls."

"Wow," he said again without moving his eye from his camera's viewfinder.

Another quick movement caught my attention as I scanned around, this time on the ground, about five metres away. I watched instinctively as a ginger shape rustled away between fallen sticks, stones and dead leaves. One view of the triangular head told me this was a bank vole.

"Down here," I pointed to my newfound friend, who I was sure was discovering more than he could have imagined.

"A mouse!" He called.

"No," I corrected, "that's a vole."

"A pole?"

"No, a vole, a bank vole, I believe."

"Not a mouse,"

"No, a vole has a very triangular head, little or no neck and a much shorter tail."

"Wow!" he repeated, changing the position to obtain more photos.

After another relatively uneventful thirty minutes, I was about to leave when a familiar sight recaptured my interest. A small brown creature with a thin curved beak and white underparts seemingly scurrying up a tree – a treecreeper.

I lifted my camera and took a couple of photos before letting the other man know what I had seen.

"There is a treecreeper," I explained, pointing it out.

"A what?"

"Treecreeper."

"T r e e c r e e p e r," he repeated, almost spelling the name out, "it's just like a mouse the way it runs up that trunk."

"It is, and it can't run down," I explained.

"Can't it? Why not?"

"It wasn't designed that way to come back down the tree; it was created only to go up it."

"How strange."

"Indeed."

"Like us, it is fearfully and wonderfully made."

"Why does it walk up tree trunks."

"Looking for food. It eats spiders, grubs and insects."

"Wow, how incredible. What were the names of all these birds again? I need to remember when I download my photos. The first little red, brown and grey bird was a redskin, right?"

Finally, I got him to write the correct names down on his phone and left him, hopefully, a little more enlightened about the natural world about him.

The nuthatch, the other little woodland bird, beats the treecreeper not only in the looks stakes but also in its ability to roam freely up and back down a tree trunk in search of sustenance. It is an incredibly impressive bird for its reasonably small size with a very powerful-looking beak.

I enjoy walking, but not at a sprint. I like to take my time and enjoy all that is around me. I'll maybe stop, look through my binoculars and carry on unless I see something of interest, then my camera comes out. When walking a distance, I usually enjoy the downhill paths best

On one occasion, while walking in County Wicklow, Ireland, things were slightly different! The path was waymarked and circular, measuring, so it said four kilometres. We set off on a gentle path that quickly became steeper and steeper, meandering through woods, felled forest and towards a ridge that, to me, never seemed to get any closer. Finally, hot, tired, agitated and a long way behind my wife and daughter, I reached the summit. The walk felt much further than four kilometres.

Karen phoned as I crossed the ridge, "We have taken the shortcut down the steps marked by a red post."

I finally found the post and looked at the set of steps cut into the forest floor that seemed to descend without end. I thought going down would be an easy affair, but no, it seemed worse on my legs, knees, back, and body than walking up the path. Every step down appeared to make another part of my body ache. I bypassed the steps and walked alongside them on the forest floor. After slipping a couple of times, I resumed the painful steps.

The downhill sections can be tough going in Christian life; that is because the Christian should never be on a downward road! Going down, in the Bible, speaks of danger, defeat and distance. In Luke Ch10 v30, the Lord Jesus tells the story known as 'The Good Samaritan,' about a man who '*Went down from Jerusalem to Jericho*'. As he travelled, he was attacked by robbers who left him nearly dead. Although seemingly an easier path, the downward route usually leads away from God and safety.

As I discovered, negotiating the downward flight of steps in the Wicklow woods, going downhill, can be a painful experience. It is interesting that despite its duller colouring, the treecreeper is the best example of the two birds for a believer to follow as it's consistent in that it's always going up. The nuthatch, on the other hand, will wander both up and down.

The apostle Paul told us about his desire, ***'Forgetting those things which are behind, and reaching forth unto those things which are before, I press toward the mark for the prize of the high calling of God in Christ Jesus'. (Philippians Ch3 v13-14).***

A hymn writer put it this way.

I'm pressing on the upward way
New heights I'm gaining every day
Still praying as I onward bound
Lord, plant my feet on higher ground

As I have wandered through woodlands and forests looking for the exuberant nuthatch or the entertaining treecreeper, I have often wondered if the treecreeper is jealous. Does it look at the nuthatch asking, 'Why do I have to go up the trees when you can go up and down?" Life must seem a little unfair for the dull, upward travelling treecreeper.

The Christian life may come across as dull to those not saved. While we carefully make our way along the road to Heaven, some Christians may be tempted to look at people in the world, envying their success in one way or another. As a Christian, it is very easy to have such a view of others if we take our eyes off the Lord.

There is a challenging verse in the Bible that says, ***'I am crucified with Christ: nevertheless I live; yet not I, but Christ liveth in me: and the life which I now live in the flesh I live by the faith of the Son of God, who loved me, and gave Himself for me' (Galatians Ch2 v20).***

A Christian should live a crucified life, but what is a crucified life? One man has helpfully pointed out that someone about to be crucified – die on a cross – was marked by three features.

They had no future plans of their own.
They were never going back.
They were always facing in one direction.

This sums up the busy little treecreeper's behaviour as it continually makes its way up one tree trunk after another. It is how Christians should be, always looking up, always moving towards Heaven and always ensuring their plans are God's plans.

Nuthatch

DIVING DOLPHINS
– SENSATIONAL ENCOUNTERS

Fascinating Facts
Dolphins usually swim slowly but can reach 30mph when required. Dolphins possess a large vocabulary using a variety of clicks, squeaks, groans, squawks, whistles, barks and yelps to communicate. The mother feeds her calf on milk for up to eighteen months, squirting it into its mouth as it suckles while swimming alongside.

The Moray coast and Cromarty Firth in Scotland are great places to see dolphins. Taking a visit for one of our holidays, we hoped to see something of the dolphin pods in the area.

We stayed in a little bungalow in a superb location overlooking the Cromarty Firth. Things did not start well on this holiday. Our daughter had seen her bedroom, rushed in, leapt on the bed, heard a loud crack and almost ended up on the floor. Her bed had broken!

Then, early on the first morning, I was woken by a strange vibrating feeling that affected the whole house. I lay still, trying to work out what was going on. Eventually, I clambered out of bed to check on the washing machine. It wasn't on. I looked at the boiler, nothing untoward there. This deep rumbling vibration seemed to grow more intense every second. I was at a loss as to what was causing it. I decided to look outside. Pulling back the curtains in the lounge, I saw a vast white building floating past about one hundred metres from us. It took a few moments to register the moving object as a ship – a passenger liner, and it was huge. The vibrations from its massive engines were coming right across the Firth and into our accommodation. It was a very unusual experience.

The obvious must-do of the holiday was to take a boat trip to see the dolphins. We were very excited when we had booked the trip and paid the fare to travel on a fast rib boat. We clambered into the boat on the chosen day and securely fastened ourselves into the seats. The captain was a woman who kindly provided a continual commentary as we passed various sites along the trip, all the while supposedly visiting all the dolphin's hotspots. Sometimes as we moved about the Cromarty Firth, she let the boat go at some speed and often, my heart was in my mouth as we skimmed close to the oil rigs towed into the Firth from the oil fields of the North Sea for service and repair. The giant metal structures towered out of the water high above us like some martian invaders depicted in a science fiction novel.

We sped from Cromarty towards Invergordon and Jemimaville. Still no sign of dolphin activity despite assurances from our captain that they were always around. We slowed down and stopped alongside a large buoy when heading back towards the narrow channel that leads from the Cromarty Firth into the much bigger Moray Firth.

"Beneath us," the captain expounded as if trying to divert our attention from the dolphins' lack of appearance, "is the wreck of HMS Natal; this ship blew up on 30th December 1915 with the loss of nearly four hundred lives." She explained that the explosion occurred internally, perhaps from faulty ammunition, and the ship capsized and sank in five minutes.

Off we set again, with time rapidly running out for seeing the dolphins who, I surmised, were probably having a merry time hiding beneath the water as we hunted for them above. We ventured out into Moray Firth without the sniff of any form of underwater creature. An odd gull rose from the waves here and there as we sped towards them but still no dolphins.

"Time to head back, I'm afraid," our captain informed us as she turned the craft around to follow the coastline back towards the village of Cromarty we had left nearly two hours earlier. I knew Karen and Grace were as disappointed as I was that we had not encountered these beautiful marine mammals.

As we once again approached the deep narrow channel between the two firths, I prayed, a rather unhopeful prayer, that we might see just a glimpse of a dolphin or maybe two. Suddenly not one or two but a whole pod broke the water's surface directly in front of the rib boat.

The captain throttled back as we came to a standstill, each passenger enthralled with camera in hand at the spectacle of perhaps twenty-five dolphins racing through the waters around the boat. Then as if on-demand, the dolphins jumped maybe ten feet into the air just ahead of where we had stopped. It was a breathtaking display as we hardly knew where to look; at the nearer creatures swimming close to the boat or the performers leaping and jumping in tandem a little ahead of us. It was a thrilling experience to be part of and something we talked about for weeks later.

Anyone wanting to watch any type of wildlife will need patience and perseverance. Going to the right places to see the right thing is essential. There is no point looking for a dolphin in an inland lake or looking for a puffin in your garden! You need to know where to look, just as the captain of or rib boat knew where the dolphins might be, although it took time to finally see them.

Reading the Bible is like this. It will take time and effort to gain a good understanding, and it will not be easy. As you read, you will want to memorise certain parts of the Bible or perhaps underline verses that have been a help to you.

There are, however, some vitally essential passages that, although we may not know by heart, we should know where to find them.

- Genesis chapters 1 and 2 – *Creation of all things*
- Genesis chapter 3 – *The entrance of sin into the world*
- Exodus chapter 20 and Deuteronomy chapter 5 – *The Ten Commandments*
- I Samuel chapter 17 – *David fights Goliath*
- Psalm 22 – *The foretelling of the sufferings of Christ on the cross*
- Psalm 23 – *The Lord is my shepherd*
- Isaiah chapter 53 – *The work of Christ on our behalf*
- Matthew chapters 5 to 7 – *The sermon on the mount, sometimes called the beatitudes*
- Matthew chapters 27 and 28; Mark chapters 15 and 16; Luke chapters 23 and 24; John chapters 19 and 20 – *The Lord's crucifixion and resurrection*
- John chapter 10 – *The Lord as the door, the Good Shepherd and our eternal security*
- Acts chapter 2 – *The giving of the Holy Spirit and formation of the early church*
- Colossians chapter 1 – *The supremacy of Christ*
- I Thessalonians chapter 4 – *The coming of Christ for His church (the rapture)*
- Hebrews chapter 11 – *Great men and women of faith*

Never give up reading, studying and memorising God's Word; try and make it a daily habit.

CHARMING CIRL BUNTINGS
– GOLD ON A GOLF COURSE

Fascinating Facts
The cirl bunting can be easily mistaken for its cousin, the yellowhammer (yellow head) and the reed bunting (black head). They have pink-coloured legs and feet. They do not like woods but love areas of closely cut grass and abundant hedgerows.

The more you study the birds around you, the more you will understand that most are grouped into families like finches, tits, thrushes and buntings.

I often visit the island of Jersey, located around twelve miles from the French coast. Its geographic situation attracts more unusual bird species that are rare in Britain and Ireland, and the cirl bunting is one of those fascinating birds.

During the 1800s, this delightful little bunting was relatively common across southern Britain; however, changes in farming practice, removal of hedges, and other factors resulted in the little bird being found only in a small area of Devon.

The best place to see them in Jersey is the Royal Jersey Golf Course in Grouville on the east coast. They are very localised, even on this relatively small island.

The first time I saw one was walking by the course entrance with Karen. As I looked for these colourful but rare buntings, I spotted a slight movement in the trees, and there was my first cirl bunting. It was beautiful to see its unusual black, brown, yellow, and grey plumage. Sadly, it did not stay long before flying off across the golf course.

Despite my best endeavours, it took many years before I saw one again. I had purchased a couple of helpful books, and both agreed the Royal Jersey Golf Course was the best place to see them. Thankfully the course has a right to roam across it, so you do not have to be playing golf to walk across its fairways and round its greens.

Off I set, deciding to walk its perimeter, hoping to catch sight of the tiny colourful birds. Three miles and two hours later, I was back at the car without a glimpse of one.

Having enquired in the bird hide at St Ouen's pond, a fantastic wetland area on the opposite side of the island, I was told the best place was the compost heaps alongside the golf course. Thankfully I knew them well as there was a car park right next to them.

I ventured forth armed with my new information and parked in the little car park right alongside that area the next day. I wandered back and forth between the compost heaps piled high with grass cuttings from the golf course. I saw a family of sparrows, starlings, and blackbirds along with two members of the tit family, as to the cirl buntings – not a sight!

I wandered past the compost area and onto the golf course to an area full of gorse that looked like a promising cirl bunting hotspot. Then I saw a small sign informing me that cirl buntings nested in the area, and to take extra care, I felt I was getting warm.

"Four!" Someone shouted at the top of their voice.

"Four!" Others joined in.

I feel I should have responded with 'five,' but I knew enough about golf to understand that someone shouting 'four' was warning me that a stray golf ball was heading in my direction. I covered my head with my hands as the ball landed with a thud about a metre away and stopped in the long grass. I looked up to see a golfer in the distance waving his hand. When he finally reached me, he was very apologetic!

"Sorry about that," he explained, "I sliced it a bit. It only just missed you!"

"Better luck next time," I laughed.

I moved on and continued my search for cirl buntings. Nothing was doing, and very few birds were showing. I walked about a mile from the car and came to the end of the golf course. It was time I turned around and headed back as the sun was sinking and the shadows lengthening. I had walked along the edge of the eighth hole when a little bird suddenly appeared on a gorse bush at the other side of the fairway. I lifted my binoculars to look, expecting to see another sparrow or linnet, of which there were plenty flitting around the course.

As I looked, I could see an unmistakable green and russet brown plumage, not unlike a yellowhammer but more striking. A cirl bunting! I could have cartwheeled across the fairway, apart from the fact that I have never been able to do cartwheels and am not about to start at my age!

I pulled my camera out, and checking that no one was about to hit a golf ball, I began to walk closer. The bird seemed oblivious to my efforts to creep up on it as it sat on top of the bush, occasionally giving a call. I changed my angle of approach to ensure the sun was behind me to obtain the best possible photos. On it sat as I drew closer and closer, clicking away all the time. The bunting hopped round to face me as if trying to assist me in my photographic endeavours. I took many more photos before the little bird took flight and headed back in the direction from which I had just come.

I was delighted; cirl buntings are not an everyday find. To any birdwatcher, they would be pretty special, and after being a few years since I had seen my first one, I walked back to the car quite elated. Golf balls and glorious buntings, it had been quite an afternoon.

The next day was beautiful, and, as my work finished early, I again headed for the golf course to look for cirl buntings. This time, I saw three, one that seemed relatively photogenic and the others that kept moving from bush to bush. Once again, I clicked away, enjoying every moment of being with what many birders would call a celebrity bird – a real A-lister! Sometimes, you can find something unique when looking for and observing wildlife, which was what the cirl bunting was to me.

Studying the Bible is like that. It is delightful to find something that appears to have been included just for you, and you enjoy it as if no one else had ever read it before. The Bible is the only book in the world that can work in such a way. No matter how many times you read it, you still want to go back for more, and when you do, it never disappoints to provide. No wonder the Word of God says, ***'All scripture is given by inspiration of God, and is profitable...'*** ***(2nd Timothy Ch3 v15).***

Cirl Bunting

BEGUILING SNOW BUNTINGS
– THE WINTER WONDER BIRD

Fascinating Facts
Snow buntings breed further north than any other land-based bird. Due to the cold, the female never leaves the nest during incubation, being fed by the male every fifteen minutes. When ground feeding gregariously (in a group), those at the back continually flutter ahead of the leading birds providing an ongoing 'wave' effect.

Another rare member of the bunting family is the snow bunting. As its name suggests, it comes from the colder northern countries of Greenland, Iceland and Scandinavia, where you might find a lot of snow.

It arrives on Britain and Ireland's shores around October, having braved the long flight over many miles of stormy and hostile sea from these distant lands. It is quite a feat for a small sparrow-sized bird not designed for long-distance travel.

Living close to Ramore Head in Portrush, a well-known 'hotspot' for snow buntings to visit, I thought we should have plenty of opportunities to see one.

Year after year, the various apps and web pages that detail the visits of notable rare birds would display 'Snow bunting – Ramore Head'. I would set out, when time allowed, to search the rocky headland at the extreme northern tip of Portrush that juts out like a pointing finger into the Atlantic Ocean.

Ramore Head, due to its strategic position, is one of the premier seabird watching sites in Europe. During the primary migration months of March into April and September into October, birdwatchers sit on this rocky headland for hours looking through their telescopes, counting the numbers of shearwaters, auks, and skua flying through between them and the offshore islands called the Skerries.

Each year I would walk around this windswept area searching for these lovely little visitors, and year after year would leave me disappointed. Once I heard that a cousin of the snow bunting, the lapland bunting, had been seen in the area. Up I headed, binoculars and camera in hand and floppy hat on my head, hopeful of finding another rare bunting. Once again, my efforts failed. It seemed that Ramore Head, despite all that birdwatchers said, was not profitable for me.

One morning, just after reports of the lapland buntings' arrival, I woke very early and decided to head off to the headland at around seven-thirty. There was hardly anyone about, and even the local dog walkers had not ventured out. The sight of an assortment of gulls greeted me – herring, black-headed and lesser black-backed, and the usual turnstones, sparrows and starlings that populate that place.

A surprisingly confiding and late migrating female wheatear gave me a pretty little show. I was though searching for something better and more exciting – lapland buntings. I walked, squinted, scanned, looked, listened and retraced my steps with no result. Despondently I placed my gear into the car and headed to my next port of call. I had only been away just over fifteen minutes when my 'birdguides App' flashed up, 'Ramore Head – lapland bunting!' Birdwatching can be so exasperating!

A week after my missed encounter with the laplander, I walked around the headland again, just in case it was still there. As usual, I looked in every conceivable area hoping for some sign of the rare visitor. Having consigned myself to failure again, I started back down the path towards the car. Suddenly a flash of whitish wings low down among the rocks to my left caught my eye. As soon as the bird landed, I let out a little sigh of joy – snow bunting, and what a beautiful bird it was.

Snow buntings are hardy little birds. Any bird of this size prepared to embark on an autumn trip of 2,100 miles from Canada; 1,300 miles from Greenland; 800 miles from Iceland; or even 600 miles from Scandinavia is a pretty tough cookie.

Their breeding grounds are tough too; a nest is scraped into the snow, lined with feathers and moss, or built into an ice crevice providing shelter from the elements. Snow buntings living in and around Arctic villages are happy enough to use man-made nest sites like many native birds.

Those arriving along the coasts of Britain and Ireland stay from October until April before starting back across the vast expanse of ocean to breed during the Arctic summer. The male birds leave first, up to a month before the females, possibly to ensure they find the best nesting sites before searching for a suitable mate.

One advantage of staying in a snow-hole nest is food. Insects, and believe it or not, there are plenty around its northern breeding grounds, can be incapacitated by the cold once they land on the snow. The little bird pecks them up as the breeze blows them past the snow buntings nest. I guess it is one of the original versions of home delivery!

Incredibly, such a small bird can nest and raise its young in such an inhospitable climate and then, when winter becomes too harsh, travel hundreds of miles across stormy seas to winter in our country. I believe the snow bunting's extreme behaviour offers a great challenge to all Christians. Are we prepared to do something for God even if the going gets tough and we must endure great difficulties?

History is full of the stories of great men and women who, by faith, accomplished great things for God. The lives of Jim Elliott, Wilfred Grenville, David Livingston, Dan Crawford, Fanny Crosby and Amy Carmichael are stories that every Christian should know. The Bible has its own 'heroes of faith' listed in Hebrews chapter eleven. The Bible records there the accomplishments of various people throughout the Old Testament who put their confidence in God.

Winston Churchill was Britain's Prime Minister during World War Two. In early 1941, before America joined the war, he wrote to the American President Franklin D Roosevelt, *"Put your confidence in us. Give us your faith and your blessing. We shall not fail or falter; we shall not weaken or tire. Neither the sudden shock of battle nor the long-drawn trials of vigilance and exertion will wear us down. Give us the tools, and we will finish the job."*

All Christians start the journey to Heaven well by simply placing their trust in the Lord Jesus and His finished work for salvation. God has then supplied us with the tools to finish well. We have the Holy Spirit within and the Bible to guide us. So don't give up; the Lord Jesus never gave up on us. Even before He went to the cross to die, He could say, ***'I have glorified thee on the earth: I have finished the work which thou gavest me to do'*** **(John Ch17 v4).**

In the hostile environment of a God-hating world, God will help us stand for Him and then we will glorify Him on this earth.

Snow Bunting

BATTY BATS
– MYSTERIOUS NIGHT HUNTERS

Fascinating Facts
Bats are the only flying mammals in the world, and a pipistrelle bat can devour over 3,000 insects in one night. Bats are long-lived mammals, occasionally reaching 30 years old but only producing one baby each year. They hibernate throughout winter, and most have large ears in proportion to their size.

It is a great shame that, for whatever reason, bats always seem to be linked with evil. Perhaps the vampire bat's name is responsible for this, and looking at it, it certainly is a pretty fearsome-looking little creature.

As a boy, I enjoyed going into the back garden of my house with my father at dusk. An owl used to hoot, which was magical in itself, but the bats flying here and there over the garden, chasing, catching and devouring insects, used to captivate and excite me. I always wanted to hold one and take a closer look at this mysterious creature that appears half bird and half mouse.

My first real encounter at close quarters with a bat was in Scotland. I was conducting a series of Gospel meetings, and Karen was with me. The hostess had gone away to care for her daughter, who had just had a baby, so Karen was left to keep the house and do the cooking, washing, ironing and cleaning for the husband and myself. On an occasion, just before the meeting, Karen's horrified shouts brought both master of the house and myself scurrying quickly into the kitchen as Karen made a hasty exit in the other direction.

"A bat," she exclaimed, taking a position of safety behind us two fearless men, "I think it was in the peg bag on the washing line, and I brought it in!"

We ventured cautiously into the kitchen as the little creature flew round in eccentric circles trying to determine a way out. We opened the back door to show it the way; however, it was still none the wiser.

"I have heard," I said to Karen and our host, "that if you wait for it to land and cover it with a glass jar, then place a piece of cardboard behind it, you can carry it out just like a spider."

Our host did not find this option to his liking as he flapped, waved, and shooed the frightened creature towards the door. Suddenly one of his waves neatly caught the flying bat, turned it towards the open door, and out it went.

"I thought it was you who used to play cricket," he commented as he closed his back door in triumph.

"I did," I replied, "however we used a bat to hit a ball and a hand to catch it. Hitting the bat with the hand was not part of the game!"

It was to be several years later that, once again, a similar experience took place. We were on a family holiday to celebrate the fiftieth wedding anniversary of my parents-in-law. The accommodation was delightful, the company good, and with a swimming pool, hot tub, lake and sweltering weather all week, things could not have been better.

Perhaps even more exciting was that after the first night, I discovered that bats were roosting under our windowsill in the gap between the building's outside slate walls and the internal plaster. Each night, I excused myself early from the meal table to open the window, lean out, and try to photograph the little creatures as they flew out for the night. It was thrilling to be so close to wildlife that's usually just a whirring haze in the gloom. My exploits each evening earned me the impressive title of 'batman' from my brother-in-law.

Unfortunately, on one occasion, when Karen was also in the room, things did not go to plan. My mode of leaning over the window sill from where the bats left the roost and launched out into the evening skies disrupted the intention of one bat. It flew off, circled back, and, flying over the top of my head, went straight into our bedroom!

Karen saw it before I even had a chance to react and dived headlong with a little shriek under the duvet, leaving me to confront the disorientated bat.

I knew I had to use my plan and wait until it landed. It did, on the headboard of the bed right above where Karen lay.

"Look," I exclaimed in delight, "it's gorgeous."

"Take it out," came the muffled voice from beneath the duvet.

"But look, you may never get another chance to see a bat this close," I argued.

"I don't particularly want to see it; please just take it out," I was asked a second time.

I obtained a suitable glass, emptied the contents down the sink, and placed it over the bat. I then asked Karen to find me a piece of cardboard to slide behind the glass and hold it securely until I got to the window. Cautiously Karen emerged from her protective cover and quickly found the required cardboard.

The difficulty now was that the bat gripped the headboard's fabric so tightly I could not prize it free. Realising my dilemma, Karen once more kept a safe distance. After a lot of gentle coaxing with the card, the bat reluctantly gave up its grip and was safely secured within the glass's confines with the cardboard covering the top. Only then did Karen take the briefest of looks into the glass at the captured mammal.

I took it to the window, and to ensure we did not have a repeat performance, I lowered it so that just my hands holding the glass were through the small gap to the outside. I removed the cardboard, and out flew the bat to join, somewhat belatedly, its friends for the evening 'fly' hunt across the lake.

My most recent encounter was in South Wales, staying with a most delightful gentleman in his early nineties who I had known for over thirty years.

When I lived in South Wales, he and his wife kindly asked me for tea when I was preaching in the Gospel Hall they attended. However, my parents, who were not Christians, were visiting me, so I declined, explaining that I would just turn up for the meeting.

"Oh, that's not a problem, Rob," he exclaimed, "bring them as well."

And so I did. My parents came to tea and listened to the preaching at the Gospel Hall about how the Lord Jesus loved them, died for them and provided a way for them to Heaven if only they would repent of their sin and trust Christ as their Saviour. I have always been thankful that this delightful couple gave my parents this opportunity to hear the Gospel again.

So I was pleased to stay with this gentleman some thirty years later and take some children's meetings, speak in the local school, and conduct a local library talk. One night as we climbed the stairs to bed, a bat flew past me on the landing.

"We have a bat," I said, trying to suppress my feeling of great excitement.

"Is your window open, Rob?" he enquired.

Now I have never enjoyed having my name shortened. My father called me Robert, and I like to be called Robert. I also find it difficult to shorten other people's names, such as David to Dave or Peter to Pete. However, this brother and his son, who I respect greatly, can do it and I don't mind!

"Yes, my window is open," I confessed.

"Ah," he responded unruffled, "he must have come in through that; they occasionally do if that window is open."

"If you have a glass, I think I can catch him," I replied.

The bat flew into the bathroom, and I followed it, closing the door behind me to contain it. Eventually, the poor bat landed on a cupboard door, and, glass in hand, I managed to trap it, then using a small flattened cardboard box from which I removed some tablets, I secured the bat in place and exited the bathroom in triumph.

Once safely outside, the little bat seemed reluctant to leave the safety of its glass home as it sat hunched up in the bottom, looking up at me. Eventually, it decided it was safe to take flight and left the glass to grip the side of the neighbouring house about four metres away. It sat for a couple of minutes before flapping its wings and heading out into the night.

Most bats, certainly those residing in Britain and Ireland, are relatively small, but they should never be handled without gloves. They can leave a bad wound when they bite, and a few can carry some nasty infections. The law states that bats in roost must never be disturbed, so watch but don't touch is the rule to follow.

There are seventeen species of bat known to breed on our islands. They are impossible to identify while flying unless you have a bat detector! You will sound like an expert if you can name and pronounce a few of the most common bat families.

- Common pipistrelle
- Barbastelle bat
- Long-eared bat
- Greater horseshoe bat
- Lesser horseshoe bat

You usually only ever see a bat at night time. A bat can fly about in total darkness without hitting anything. God created this little creature with a radar system (called echolocation) which is more sensitive than anything a man has invented.

We, too, by nature, love a form of darkness that shuts us out from the blessings that God can give us. When the Lord Jesus came into the world, He became 'the light of the world'. He invites everyone to come out of darkness and into His marvellous light.

Chapter eleven of the book of Leviticus provides a long list of what God terms clean and unclean animals and birds. The bat is listed as an unclean creature in verse nineteen.

Why did God tell His people to avoid the bat? Was it because it is part mammal and part bird? One moment it is flying around the sky, and the next, scratching on the ground. It seems to be neither one thing nor another. God wants us to be consistent, not one thing to one person and another to someone else. A Christian should be a person who keeps their word when they make a promise.

***Let us walk honestly, as in the day;
not in rioting and drunkenness,
not in chambering and wantonness,
not in strife and envying.
But put ye on the Lord Jesus Christ,
and make not provision for the flesh,
to fulfil the lusts thereof.***

(Romans Ch13 v13-14)

BIG BOLD BUZZARDS
– THE POLE SITTER

Fascinating Facts
Buzzards like to build a new nest each year. Although they are a large raptor (bird of prey), buzzards prefer to eat dead animals (called carrion) and dig up vast numbers of earthworms. The chick starts to call from within its egg up to three days before hatching, and parent birds never leave their young alone for the first 14 days after they hatch.

Many years ago, during another holiday in Scotland, Karen and I wanted to see a golden eagle for the first time. We were right in the middle of the Cairngorm Mountains and part way up the Findhorn Valley, prime golden eagle country. We thought we couldn't fail but see one of these impressive birds.

On our second day, we drove right into the steep-sided valley and, upon topping a hill, looked straight across at an old dead tree. Sitting on one of the branches was what we thought we were looking for, a golden eagle.

We were jubilant as I stopped the car, and we both gazed breathlessly at the rather splendid bird. In those days, the only binoculars I had were a pair borrowed from my father that dated back to the 1950s – a pair that I still have. They were big, heavy, hard to focus and difficult to hold still. We persevered, and the eagle stayed happily on the branch as we surveyed it from around two hundred metres away.

"I thought it would look bigger than that," Karen suggested.

"It's the distance," I replied, "it makes it look smaller than it is."

"Still, it isn't as big as I was expecting."

"No, no," I responded, "it may be a juvenile or a smaller adult. All birds have some variations in size."

"I'd have expected a bigger beak too."

"No! It has a fine hooked beak."

"I expected it to be darker than that."

"That's just the sun making it look lighter."

"What colour are a golden eagle's legs?"

"I don't know," I confessed, "I have never seen one before, but that's one, alright, our first golden eagle!"

It was not until three days later that I had purchased a 'bird guide' and looked through it that I began to have some doubts about my identification of the 'goldie'.

The book's pictures showed an eagle with yellow legs and claws, and ours had been a grey colour. I looked again. The beak on ours was undoubtedly smaller than the pictures in the book. I flicked through the pages, still believing our sighting was just an unusual-looking golden eagle.

Then I came to the buzzard, and my heart sank. There staring back at me from the pages of the guide, was our bird! A buzzard and not an eagle at all. How bitterly disappointing.

I decided not to reveal my misidentification to Karen. We had only been married a little over a year, and I was still trying to impress her with the bit of knowledge I had.

The next evening Karen was flicking through the bird guide and swapping the same pages back and forth; as she did so, she suddenly exclaimed, "That wasn't an eagle we saw on Monday. It looks much more like a buzzard to me!"

The spell was broken, and I had to sheepishly confess that I had come to the same sad conclusion the previous night.

Seeing a buzzard for the first time, many people make the same mistake. The birds are similar except in size, as the eagle dwarfs all our other raptors. Many people say they have seen an eagle when it has been a buzzard they have observed. The nickname occasionally given to the buzzard is the 'tourists eagle', which sums up our mistake quite well.

We are now fortunate to live in an area where often I can look out of the front of our house and see a buzzard sitting on a telegraph pole four hundred metres across a field. When out in the garden, I often watch one or two soaring on the warm air thermals, wings held straight and steady as they give a weak-sounding whistle or meowing like a cat. Our first buzzard was called Fuzz, and whenever we see one near the house, we still call it 'Fuzz the Buzz!'

Buzzards are excellent scavengers, eating animals and birds that have been killed on the road. They will also clear up other dead creatures' remains possibly left behind by their killers, such as a fox, weasel or stoat. Someone once described the buzzard as God's garbage cleaner!

Buzzards will hunt rabbits, pigeons, ducks, or some slower-moving wildlife they see from their perch high off the ground. We have often gone out on a Saturday afternoon in the car to walk the dogs and passed directly under the telegraph pole upon which Fuzz was sitting. Having walked the dogs, stopped for a coffee and returned home, the same buzzard was still sitting, waiting, in the same place. It seems to be a bird that has great patience.

I have had the pleasure of watching a buzzard hovering on several occasions, and it is fascinating seeing it trying to maintain its position. In contrast, the kestrel undertakes this feat effortlessly; the buzzard labours as if too big and bulky to keep hanging in the air indefinitely.

Whether flying, soaring, sitting, calling or hovering, the buzzard is a rather impressive-looking bird and certainly worth observing whenever possible. Often when I see this large raptor sitting watching and waiting, I'm reminded of a comical children's song I heard decades ago. It is about a farmer who is trying to scare a buzzard that is after his turkeys. In between each verse, he tries to shoo the bird away!

Children, Children, don't you hide
He can't take you for a ride
He's too skinny, and you're too wide
With a B U ZZ A R D
Thieving Turkey Buzzard

Shoo… Shoo…

B U ZZ A R D keep on flying away from me
Stop your flapping overhead
Cause I'm telling you boy that I ain't dead
With a B U ZZ A R D
Thieving Turkey Buzzard

On one occasion, Karen returned home after walking the dog and stated, "It's a pity you weren't with me, a buzzard with an injured wing fell out of the sky while driving home. It landed right in front of my car, and I stopped and watched it hop to the side of the road."

I knew exactly what had happened as soon as Karen described the encounter. The local estate held its annual pheasant shoot, and someone took a shot at the buzzard. They are slow-flying birds and have been described in the past as lazy. They seem unhurried in life, whatever they are doing, making them, sadly, an easy target for those with guns.

I gathered everything I required to rescue the injured bird and raced to the spot where Karen had seen it land. Nothing, not a sign! I looked in the hedgerows, over the wall and into the woods, all to no avail. I could only guess that those who had fired the shot had got there first and taken the bird to ensure their crime would not be discovered. The majority of wild birds in the United Kingdom are protected by law. How sad that someone wanted to break the law and cruelly take the life of such a majestic bird.

Patience! How much do you have? The buzzard seems to have loads. I confess that I am not the most patient of people. I like to be up and doing, not sitting and waiting.

Buzzard in flight

Being patient can mean waiting without complaining. Learning to be patient helps strengthen our faith and build good character. There are lots of verses in the Bible about patience; here is one of them:

Rest in the Lord, and wait patiently for Him.
(Psalm 37 v7)

This verse is much easier quoted than practised. Waiting for the Lord's answer to our prayers can be tough – I still find it so. King David, who wrote so many Psalms in the Bible, wrote:-

I waited patiently for the Lord;
and He inclined unto me, and heard my cry.
(Psalm 40 v1)

We can rest in knowing that when we pray, God hears our prayers, and an answer is on the way. I sometimes remember the words to a little song I used to listen to when I was newly saved:-

Many times I'm bowed beneath a heavy load.
On bended knees to God, a prayer I prayed.
As I knelt there on the floor.
He reminded me once more.
That the answer was already on the way.

Oh yes, the answers on the way this I know
Jesus said it, I believe it, and it's so
Our Heavenly Father knows our needs before we pray
And we can rest assured the answers on the way!

God always answers our prayers but not always in the way we want. He either answers yes or no or says wait. Therefore, we must learn the sometimes hard lesson of waiting patiently for Him!

THRILLING TIT FAMILY
– SURPRISINGLY SHOCKING SECRETS

Fascinating Facts
In America, many members of the tit family are called chickadees or titmice. They often move through woodlands in mixed flocks to stay safe and watch out for danger. Tits are considered, after corvids and parrots, some of the most highly intelligent birds in the world. The long tailed tit, although not a true family member is closely related.

What do you do when you do not have enough material to write about just one bird? Call the family together. So that is what I will do here with the tit family. They are lovely little birds that are probably an introduction to bird watching for many. All members of this dexterous family have an appeal; whether it is swinging upside down from feeders or trees, seeking some tasty morsel or their constant coming and going to their nesting sites, each bird has a character of its own.

BLUE TIT

Surprisingly this common and brightly coloured little bird has a pretty gruesome secret; it is the executioner bird. Like me, if you enjoy history, you may have read of those in days gone by who were beheaded. It was a gruesome affair, and many bloodthirsty people came to stand around the scaffold to watch the unfortunate person die.

I am old enough to remember the days when the milkman would deliver the milk to each house on his round in the early hours of the morning. Many drove an electric milk float that was quiet so as not to wake people as it passed silently along the street whilst householders were still asleep in bed.

Several records exist of blue tits following the milkman, knowing they could peck the bottles' gold or silver foil tops and drink the cream. Often as a teenager, when I left the house at six-thirty in the morning to do my paper round, I would discover that the blue tits had already visited our milk bottles.

Blue tits have exclusive tastes, and they would only take the cream, not the milk. The cream was pure fat which the birds loved; however, the milk contained lactose, making the blue tits ill. With much of the creamy fat content removed, the introduction of semi-skimmed and skimmed milk helped stop the blue tits' legendary habit.

Now back to the executions. Blue tits feed their young on caterpillars and lots of them. If you ever see a caterpillar, you will notice that it can munch through many leaves in a day. It has jaws and teeth, and if fed alive to a young blue tit, it could give it a nasty bite and injure the young bird. Therefore, the adult will turn executioner and bite off the caterpillars' heads; this removes the jaws and so protects its young from harm. Blue tits have also been known to remove caterpillars' guts to help protect the young birds from possible harmful poisonous toxins that might be lurking there.

GREAT TIT

The familiar great tit, like its smaller relative, the blue tit, also hides a shocking secret. It harbours sinister desires to be another bird altogether. It wants to join that select band of flying killers… the raptors! Maybe that is why it wears that black and white balaclava look over its head to make it appear more of an outlaw?

The great tit will occasionally attack and eat other creatures, smaller birds than itself, small lizards and frogs, and even bats while they

Great Tit

roost. So one of the most common visitors to your garden bird table may well have a guilty history!

They are intelligent birds, too; when feeding their young, they determine which size of a caterpillar is required according to the size of the chick. The parent birds work hard to provide their young with appropriate-sized food, large caterpillars for the larger chicks and smaller bite-sized ones for smaller chicks.

COAL TIT

Catch it if you can! All members of the tit family are constantly and energetically on the move. They hardly seem to rest as they grab a seed or two from the feeders in the garden and then hurry away into the cover and safety of some dense bush. However, the coal tit takes this behaviour to extremes as it dives onto the table, picks up a seed, and then shoots away before returning less than a minute later to repeat the operation.

Coal Tit

What is it up to, and why the rush? The coal tit is the tit most likely to be bullied by other larger family members. It, therefore, has developed a 'grab and run' technique to protect its food supplies. Once it has taken something from the bird feeders, it shoots off to hide it before it is bullied into handing its prize over to the larger great tits or blue tits. It's a bird on the go and constantly having to look over its shoulders in case its cousins are around.

LONG TAILED TIT

This bird, without a doubt, is my favourite member of this species, even though it actually belongs to a different family group.

I still get a buzz when I see them moving through the tree canopy or suddenly appearing en masse on my bird feeders. It would be up at the top of my list of all-time favourite birds too. There is very little to dislike about the long-tailed tit.

Long Tailed Tit

They are nearly always seen in flocks flitting around, watching for danger and seeking food. They are just a joy to watch.

It is their nest that impresses me. What a magnificent and complex structure it is. When completed, it forms a dome that has taken three weeks to make using over six thousand individual pieces of material, including spider webs. The inside is lined with around two thousand feathers. The question is, where do long-tailed tits obtain so many feathers? You may be amazed at the answer. Dead birds! Yes, you did read that correctly; long-tailed tits can find dead birds and pluck their feathers off their bodies to line their nests. It is a case of one bird dying to feather another bird's nest!

During winter, many long-tailed tits will huddle together inside this intricate nest. The dominant birds will occupy the centre to receive the most heat, with subordinate birds continually moving around the nest's outer wall swapping places with other birds to warm up. This must be the avian equivalent to central heating!

CRESTED TIT

I have not seen a crested tit despite often looking for them during my many visits to the Scottish Highlands. You will not find them anywhere other than in the pine forests around the Cairngorms National Park. Many fortunate people living in that beautiful scenic area are privileged to have crested tits visiting their gardens.

Once again, here is a bird with a horrible secret. It enjoys fresh food and likes storing it up when winter is harsh, and food is scarce. Insects, and especially spiders, are its favourite diet. Therefore, the crested tit catches a spider and incapacitates it by pulling off some of its legs before glueing it with its saliva or even wrapping it in spider silk in a safe storage area whilst the poor creature is still alive. As a result, the insect is kept fresh for longer. Now comes the tricky part. The 'crestie' cannot remember where it has placed its hoard. However, it forages in the same areas of its territory day after day, so eventually, it comes across its stashed catch and enjoys a much-needed meal.

WILLOW TIT AND MARSH TIT

Most readers will never have seen either of these birds unless you are a keen birdwatcher. If you came across them, you would struggle to know which is which because they are so similar. Until the year 1900, the birds were considered the same species.

The best way to separate them is by their songs, which are different. Now comes another difficulty, what if, like me, you don't know their songs? Then I suggest you are in a considerable degree of trouble!

A few years ago, I was sitting in a hide overlooking a lake. Between the water and myself was a wonderfully natural bird table. It had been scattered with seeds and nuts that a host of birds were coming to take, blue tits, great tits, coal tits, long-tailed tits, chaffinches, nuthatch, house sparrow, and finally, marsh tits.

Marsh Tit

A family was sitting close by, and the father pointed out all the familiar birds to his children. When the marsh tit arrived, he pointed it out and said, "Oh, there is something unusual; it's a coal tit without the white stripe on the back of its head."

I ignored the father's comments, initially being quite impressed with the extent of his knowledge and excitedly snapped away at the marsh tit, knowing it was something I had not seen for years. When the bird visited the second time, and the father again informed his children that it was a strange-looking coal tit. I felt I had to straighten the record.

"I hope you don't mind me saying, but that little bird is a marsh tit."

"Oh! What did you call it?"

"A marsh tit."

"Never heard of it," he replied in his Birmingham accent.

"A woodland bird," I explained, trying to sound like an expert, "it's often confused with a willow tit which looks like its twin; they are so similar."

"Really, and this is the marsh tit is it? How do you know which is which?"

"One has a slightly glossier black crown, one is somewhat more unkempt, and they have different songs."

"Ohh, well, you learn something new every day."

"Did you hear what this gentleman said?" he questioned, regaining his children's attention. "This is not a coal tit without a white stripe on its head, but a marsh tit that I have never heard of."

Eventually, they left the hide when the patience of his two young charges started to wane.

"Thanks," he said with a wave of his hand, "marsh tit, I'll remember that one from now on."

I confess I was a little chuffed to have sounded so confident in identifying it so well. I did not tell the man that about ten metres from the hide, I had read an information sheet telling me that marsh tits resided in the woods! Without that information, I would not have known whether it was a marsh tit or a willow tit! It's a good idea to pay attention to information boards!

What a variety of interesting characters there are in this unique family. The would-be killer birds, birds that like to feather their nests, the busy-as-a-bee birds, those who steal from the milk of human kindness and the almost identical twin birds. What a branch of fascinating lives.

People in the world are just the same. We are marked by great variety. Some are good, some turn bad, some are normal, some busy, some idle and a myriad in-between. The one common thing about everyone is that all have sinned. Sin is rebellion against God.

It says, 'I want my way, I want to do my thing, and I don't care about what God thinks'. We are all guilty at some time of that attitude.

The good news of the Gospel is for everyone without exception; murderers, thieves, business people, bullies, the bullied, family members, rich, poor, good or bad. How wonderful is this glad message?

The Bible tells us that Christ ***'died for all' (2nd Corinthians Ch5 v15).*** As a result of His work on the cross, all can ***'repent and turn to God' (Acts Ch26 v20)*** and ***'trust in the living God' (1st Timothy Ch4 v10).*** This happens when we ***'believe on the Lord Jesus Christ' (Acts Ch16 v31)***, and we are saved!

Long Tailed Tit

STUNNING SLAVONIAN GREBES – SCOTTISH GLORY

Fascinating Facts
The rare titicaca grebe that lives on the border of Peru and Bolivia has such short wings that it cannot fly. Grebes have impressive feet with broad individual toes shaped like flower petals, and this design helps them swim through the water and perform their incredible dance moves. Slavonian grebes eat their feathers, which remain in the stomach, acting as a filter to hold fish bones together until they can be digested.

You will not come across a Slavonian grebe every day; it is not even a bird you will see every year. It is very rare, but when in its summer plumage, it is a magnificent water bird. They breed only in a few select areas of the Scottish Highlands.

We had an excellent opportunity to see them shortly after we married.

One late spring, we were offered a two-week holiday in a remote location of the Scottish Highlands; we were very excited.

We set off on the seven-hour journey on a Friday. In those days, we owned a Nissan Serena people carrier. It was great on seats and accommodation but seriously underpowered, being a car without a turbo. Even on a motorway, climbing hills required a good fast run and then a change of gears to fourth and sometimes down to third to negotiate the incline. A Grand Prix car, it certainly wasn't.

We finally arrived at our destination. The location couldn't have been better, with heather-clad mountains all around and a loch stretching out in the distance over which the occasional osprey flew, and three quaint log cabins nestled amongst deciduous and pine trees, one of which was to be our home for the two weeks.

Tired after a full day of journeying in our somewhat sluggish vehicle, we went inside the allocated cabin. We soon realised delightful though the place was, it needed a little refreshing and tidying up as it obviously hadn't been aired for a few months. The carpets needed vacuuming, and the kitchen work surfaces were a little grubby.

Karen is always pragmatic, "Let's go to bed, get up early and spend tomorrow morning cleaning the place," she suggested. As I had no desire to set to with vacuum, mops, dusters and cloths that night, I readily agreed. The bed looked nice and clean, so we looked forward to a good night's sleep.

The following day we got up and began cleaning through the lodge. In her exuberance for straightening up the place, Karen had the two of us give it a thorough cleansing that I am sure it had not had in a long time. We scrubbed, cleaned, mopped, vacuumed, dusted, and washed until eleven.

Anyone who knows me is aware that I like my tea. So after our hard work, we put the kettle on for a brew with the Yorkshire tea we had brought. After filling the kettle, I noticed some insects floating inside as I put the lid on. I tipped all the water out, and as a result, we washed through all the pots, pans and dishes in the cupboards.

Once everything was cleaned, dried, and put away in the freshly wiped-out cupboards, we tried again for a cup of tea. I could hardly believe it when I looked into the kettle to find another creature inside.

"How did that get there?" I questioned.

"It looks like a prawn," Karen said, looking closer.

Finally, we read the instructions for the cabin. The water was pumped into the house from a well, and living in the well were some freshwater shrimps. This meant that every time we turned on the water, we had to run it through a sieve to catch these errant creatures.

With a large mug of freshly brewed tea in hand, I sat down on the sofa to relax for the first time. As the cushions took my weight, I suddenly fell right through and landed on the floor. Hot tea went everywhere, over me, the sofa and across the floor. Frantically I attempted to extricate myself from the settee's frame as Karen surveyed the resulting scene of devastation in amusement!

When finally back on my feet and using a tea towel to dry off, I pulled out the cushions to see why I had ended up on the ground. The wooden framed two-seater was one of the old-fashioned affairs from a few decades previous. It boasted a series of long elasticated straps crossing the frame to support the cushions. Over time these had perished and required to be replaced. However, someone had placed several collapsed cardboard boxes across the three remaining straps to extend its life. They might have supported a person of average build, but someone around six feet six inches was a different proposition!

Four days into the holiday, Karen discovered that suddenly we had no hot water. I checked fuses, switches, and electrical connections as best I could but could not find the problem. Finally, in desperation, we contacted the owners.

Two cold baths later, a plumber arrived to inform us that the water heater had packed up. It took another day of cold baths before he returned to fit the required part. The rest of the stay passed in relative dullness in comparison!

We walked the short distance from the cabin to the loch side most days to observe the rather splendid brightly coloured Slavonian grebes. These rare birds are more often seen in winter when up to five hundred visit our coastline. This loch in Scotland opposite our cabin was where most of the fifty known breeding pairs were nesting. It was a wonderful place to be with a beautiful bird to see.

One of the identifying characteristics of the Slavonian grebe is its red eyes. These unusually coloured eyes have led to nicknames such as 'devil diver' and 'water witch'. In America, its yellow feather tufts on either side of its head have given it the name 'horned grebe'. These are not the kindest descriptions of a rather unique bird.

All grebes are fantastic birds and well worth seeing. You are most likely to spot the great crested grebe, the largest and most elegant of them all. I have been fortunate enough to see and photograph its synchronised courtship dance, concluding with the birds passing each other pondweed as a seal of their bond.

The 'great crest' is an imposing and striking bird in its summer plumage, displaying its white, russet and black crest. Unfortunately, the Victorians liked the bird's feathers and persecuted it nearly to extinction to adorn their scarves, hats and coats with 'grebe fur!' Thankfully, for the grebes, times have changed.

Great Crested Grebes

The other grebe, any observer, should come across is the little grebe. This tiny cutie is often called the 'dabchick;' however, in Lancashire, they occasionally call it 'foot in the bottom' because its feet are placed so far back behind its body. This arrangement provides it with excellent swimming ability but makes it a clumsy bird when on a few occasions, it walks on land. It reminds me of a small football covered in feathers with a head and neck stuck on one end. When seen, it certainly has the 'Ooooh' factor, as it looks cute and cuddly.

Little Grebe

Standing by a lakeside, camera in hand, I have often attempted to photograph these highly energetic little waterbirds. I have set up the camera zoomed, and then... suddenly, the grebe has disappeared without a trace. Initially, someone who had never seen one before might think they were going mad. You see a bird, lift your binoculars or camera to take a look and... it has vanished. The little grebe is a nervous character who can suddenly dive without sound and leave hardly a ripple on the water's surface. If it suspects danger, it will submerge and, once below the water, will swim quickly and powerfully towards the nearest vegetation, where it can remain quite still with only its beak sticking out of the water, allowing it to breathe.

One feature all grebes have in common is their nests. They float! You could never say that grebes were great engineers. They often seem to throw a few twigs, reeds, different types of grass and feathers together, anchor them onto nearby vegetation, and seemingly hope for the best. They don't bother too much about foundations. Of course, there are records of eggs falling into the water and nests and chicks washed away in fierce spring storms.

Foundations! Every house, office and building needs them to stand. Years ago, my father-in-law had an extension built onto his house. The builders started digging for the foundation but, having excavated six feet, found nothing solid on which to build.

"Keep digging," my father-in-law told them.

At ten feet down, they called again, "Still no firm ground."

"Keep digging!"

Finally, at a depth of eighteen feet, they hit the rock and commenced to build. Without digging so deep, the extension would not have been stable and would have started to sink and break away from the house very quickly. Good firm foundations in life are vital.

The Bible has quite a bit to say about foundations. One of Job's three so-called friends said this:-

Behold, God put no trust in His servants; and His angels He charged with folly: How much less in them that dwell in houses of clay, whose foundation is in the dust, which are crushed before the moth?

(Job Ch4 v18-19)

Eliphaz was trying to tell Job that even a little moth could cause a house built on a foundation of dust to collapse.

One day, the Lord Jesus told this searching parable about two men who decided to build two different houses.

Whosoever cometh to Me, and heareth My sayings, and doeth them, I will shew you to whom he is like: he is like a man which built an house, and digged deep, and laid the foundation on a rock: and when the flood arose, the stream beat vehemently upon that house, and could not shake it: for it was founded upon a rock. But he that heareth, and doeth not, is like a man that without a foundation built an house upon the earth; against which the stream did beat vehemently, and immediately it fell; and the ruin of that house was great.

(Luke Ch6 v47-49)

Those who listen to and obey the Lord Jesus's words have a foundation to rest upon during this life and one that will provide eternal security in Heaven. Have you listened to His words and acted upon His commands to trust Him as the only Saviour from sin?

Nevertheless the foundation of God standeth sure, having this seal, The Lord knoweth them that are His. And, Let every one that nameth the name of Christ depart from iniquity.

(2nd Timothy Ch2 v19)

HELPFUL HEDGEHOGS
– PRICKLY, POINTED AND PECULIAR

Fascinating Facts
Their name suits them well as they often nest under hedges and can snort similar to a hog (pig). Their eyes are made to see at night; however, they primarily use their ability to hear and smell to search out prey. They are loners, only pairing up with other hedgehogs to mate. Baby hedgehogs are born spineless; however, white spines begin to appear within hours, and a week later, brown ones become predominant.

In the introduction, I described our ministrations to 'Hayley,' a sick hedgehog we attempted to help, sadly, without success.

Thinking back, I cannot recall when I saw my first hedgehog. It must have been in the house where I lived with my parents for nearly seventeen years. The garden was long and had several mature trees at the bottom, forming a woodland canopy between different gardens. Perhaps I should say that it did until one neighbour felled all his trees, spoiling the 'nature highway'. There was a marked decrease in visiting squirrels after removing those trees.

Once Karen and I moved to our second house and having observed the occasional hedgehog in the locality, I obtained plans for a hedgehog house and set to work. The instructions were pretty basic and, therefore, easy for a ham-fisted amateur carpenter like myself to follow. The structure involved producing a box about thirty centimetres square by twenty centimetres high with an entrance tunnel around fifty centimetres long. Once completed, I stupidly covered the whole design in a substantial piece of tarpaulin to keep it dry and buried it under a mound next to an oak tree growing in our garden. I had never considered that the box might require to be cleaned out after use.

A couple of months later, I saw a hedgehog outside our house. I quickly obtained some gloves (don't try picking one up without wearing some), caught it and took it to try and interest it in the new home I had made for them. I put it down near the entrance, and without any hesitation, it ran straight along the entrance tunnel.

How remarkable! Most animals and birds are very cautious about approaching something new in case it represents danger. They undertake a lot of sniffing, prodding, searching and checking before doing anything else. To my mind, diving in without a thought was highly unusual. I decided to watch the hog house from the security and warmth of our dining room.

Half an hour later, I was excited to see the hedgehog emerge, followed by another! They had already searched, evaluated, approved and taken up residence in the little house. That summer, we watched as the parents left the nest each evening to feed. We lent a helping hand by putting out a little dog food each night, before eventually discovering that you can purchase hedgehog food from some garden centres and pet shops.

On one occasion, we watched open-mouthed as the parents tentatively brought three young 'hogs' out of the homemade house and into the garden for the first time. This was exciting! The efforts involved in building a single hedgehog nesting chamber had paid off. We had seen our first family born, and now they roamed happily around our garden.

To assist visiting 'hogs', I cut a small ten-centimetre by ten-centimetre hole at the bottom of our fence that opened onto a public footpath leading into the woods. This footpath was bordered on either side by brambles, nettles and tree roots, all ideal foraging areas for inquisitive hedgehogs looking for spiders, beetles, earthworms and grubs.

Following the success of the first hedgehog house, I set to with thoughts of the possibility of becoming an accomplished hog house property developer and made a second. I had read that hedgehogs will only ever use a nest site once, and to encourage them to stay in your garden, you should put out at least two. Eventually, with my daughter's help, we had five hedgehog homes, with names like 'prickle palace,' 'spikes shelter,' and 'hogs house'. Our daughter, clever and artistic, unlike her father, made excellent little nameplates for each abode. We even presented an extra house we had made to the local hedgehog hospital. We do not see as many hedgehogs now, as we did when living in Yorkshire, and we miss them. Despite having three state-of-the-art hedgehog houses in our garden, we have not had a sighting in eight years. Their inquisitive nature of shuffling around under bushes, in flower borders and across the lawn made them a joy to watch.

Of course, we were not averse as a family to stopping the car and jumping out to assist a hedgehog in its perilous pursuit to cross some road or other. I still keep leather gloves in the car for such an eventuality or rescuing other creatures. It is always best to be prepared, and these gloves have come in handy for collecting dead animals that have been unfortunate enough to fall victim to cars when crossing the road. Such creatures are usually taken home and buried somewhere in the garden. Our present home is the graveyard of a family of ducklings, three juvenile ducks, a badger, a myriad of birds, plus our rabbit called Fluffy and our cavalier King Charles spaniels, Barney and Wellington! If we ever move, the dogs and rabbit will have to be exhumed and taken with us!

Hedgehogs are pretty amazing characters. Their name suits them perfectly as they like nothing more than to be scratching around for food under the protection of some hedge or other. They also make a pretty impressive snorting noise, like a pig. As pigs are often called hogs, the name fits perfectly.

Each hedgehog has around five thousand spines on their bodies, which are generally replaced with new ones yearly. That is quite an impressive amount, and they are indeed rather sharp. Someone once tried to tell me that hedgehogs could burst the tyres on a car when it ran over them. Although motorists might take more care if this was the case, I think it's highly improbable. I have read more reliable accounts of dead hedgehogs being responsible for popping bicycle tyres when cyclists run over their bodies. That I can understand.

Many people attempt to help hedgehogs they see visiting their gardens by putting milk out for them. Hedgehogs are allergic to lactose (something found in milk), making them sick despite the well-meaning intention. Putting out a water bowl and some dog or cat food would be far better. Most good garden centres and a few bigger pet shops now sell a specially prepared hedgehog mix. If you put food out, don't put out too much, and check who is eating it. Although rats are interesting creatures and surprisingly clean little rodents, most people would not want to encourage them into their gardens.

If you can get a little closer to a hedgehog, and they can be very obliging, you may see some ugly, grey, pea-sized growths on its body, especially around its eyes and neck. These are ticks that are pretty nasty tiny parasitic insects feeding off the hedgehog's blood.

Initially, ticks look like tiny spiders. They attach themselves to the host, climb in among the fur, and bite into the flesh to suck its blood. The grey blob is like a small balloon that expands as it fills with blood. A healthy hedgehog can usually carry a couple of these horrible insects; however, if you see a hog with more than a couple of ticks attached, it is probably a sign that the poor little thing needs some help. Ticks carry lyme disease, which can affect people, so be careful they don't take a bite at you!

You can purchase 'tick pulls' from the vets; however, using these requires a little practice; otherwise, you can kill the tick but leave the head part still attached to the poor hedgehog. These will go septic and cause your spiky friend more harm. It would be best to take the hedgehog to a sympathetic vet or look up a hedgehog rescue hospital near you. You would be surprised how many are run by people who have a care and concern for these enigmatic little characters. They will have the expertise to find, remove and kill all the ticks present and provide aftercare for the hog to ensure it is as fit as possible before releasing it back into the wild.

Ticks remind me of sin! God loves all sinners, people like you and me; however, He hates our sin. Sins are the wrong things we do because we are born sinful. Most people cannot help but tell lies, swear, think evil thoughts, lose their temper, and the list goes on. Like the tick on the hedgehog, sin starts small and almost so insignificant that you'd hardly notice it was there at all. Just look at how easily sin can spread in your life – bad thoughts become bad words, then bad deeds.

At first, no one can see or know about it; then, suddenly, sin becomes visible to all. God, of course, sees and knows everything.

The heart is deceitful above all things and desperately wicked: who can know it? I the Lord search the heart, I try the reins, even to give every man according to his ways, and according to the fruit of his doings.
(Jeremiah Ch17 v9-10)

These verses show us how God sees us. It does not look good at all.

I remember walking around a large electrical shop as I waited for Karen to complete her shopping in a supermarket nearby. I stopped and looked at the largest television I had ever seen. It was massive and had a price tag to go with its size. The picture was undoubtedly fuzzy as it seemed to comprise myriads of coloured dots trying to form an image but failing.

"An impressive bit of kit that," a salesman said as he ambled over to me.

"Certainly in size," I replied.

"Thinking of changing your TV?" he enquired.

"No, no, not at all; I don't have one to swap."

"We don't do trade-ins," he explained, not grasping my reply, "I meant are you thinking of replacing your current TV?"

"No, because I do not own or use a TV," I told him bluntly.

"What?" he questioned unbelievingly, "You never watch TV?"

"No, I don't, as it would waste my time."

"Oh. I have never met anyone who does not have a TV before," he responded, somewhat nonplussed.

"You learn something new every day," I told him, smiling, "I grew up with one; however, when I became a Christian, I decided I would not have one as it might waste too much time. I might also be tempted to watch something that wasn't helpful to me."

Once we had overcome that little difficulty, we turned our attention to the monster-sized television before us, and I asked him why anyone would want to buy it with such an awful picture.

"Oh, no! You see it all wrong," the assistant explained, "this is a 3D television; you need to put these glasses on to watch it properly." He handed me a pair of very cheap-looking cardboard glasses with coloured lenses. "Just pop these over your spectacles."

The picture on the giant screen before me almost magically became crystal clear as I did so. I could see a giant and fearsome-looking dinosaur running toward me. It certainly did look rather lifelike as its three-dimensional form rapidly bore down on me. Suddenly the ferocious creature leapt, and I felt it was coming right out of the set towards me. Instinctively I ducked, much to the amusement of the shop assistant.

"Good, isn't it, sir?" he commented.

I removed the cardboard glasses and looked back at the somewhat fuzzy-looking screen. "Yes, very impressive," I replied, somewhat embarrassed. "Although I do not particularly want to have dinosaurs jumping out at me in my own home, thank you. That, to me, would not make comfortable viewing of anything."

I handed the cheap-looking glasses back and bade a hasty retreat from the smiling face of the assistant. I have often wondered if they just had a short clip playing of running and leaping dinosaurs to catch unsuspecting customers like me, or was I unfortunate to watch at the wrong time?

The whole experience did get me thinking. If putting on glasses changed the image I saw, what if I could put on glasses and see things as God sees? That would be quite something. The Bible says of God - ***Thou art of purer eyes than to behold evil, and canst not look on iniquity*** **(Habakuk Ch1 v13).** We would be shocked to see how God saw sin in his holy sight. We would run from it and want to be free of it. We would be appalled at how evil, dirty and hideous it was in the presence of such holiness. Thankfully there is a wonderful cure for such uncleanness if we are prepared to humble ourselves and accept God's provision of the Lord Jesus Christ and His forgiveness.

The blood of Jesus Christ His Son cleanseth us from all sin.
(1 John Ch1 v7)

Once you are saved, the power of sin over you is completely destroyed, and you can, with the help of God, live a righteous life.

Hedgehog family

CURIOUS CORVID FAMILY
– BORING BUT BRILLIANT

Fascinating Facts
The raven is the largest songbird in the world, not that it sings a very tuneful song! Some members of the corvid family can stash up to 30,000 seeds and remember with over 90% accuracy where they placed them. All corvids have large beaks, strong feet and broad wings and most mate for life.

If someone surveyed people's favourite birds, I am relatively confident that robin and puffin would be in the top place and equally sure that some member or members of the corvid family would come last. What are corvids? Many people often lump them together as 'crows' simply because they do not take the time to learn which is which.

Across Britain and Ireland, there are seven members of this rather interesting family. Five of these birds are 'black' birds, one is black and white, whilst the last is surprisingly one of our more colourful birds.

JACKDAW

The energetic jackdaw is, perhaps surprisingly, one of my favourite birds. It visits our bird table daily and is highly entertaining as it attempts to feed through the plastic mesh I have placed around the platform to keep feral pigeons and stock doves from hogging all the food. The bird table also has an adaptation I added to assist our local pheasants. A broom handle is screwed underneath, extending two feet on either side, making a prominent perch. Upon this, the jackdaws often sit patiently, waiting their turn to peck through the mesh and pick up the loose seeds lying around the table.

There are two striking things about the jackdaw: its grey head and bright eye, which set it apart from other corvids. The eye is especially notable and is used to scare off would-be predators at the nest site. Imagine looking into a dark cupboard and seeing nothing but a pair of scary eyes looking back at you through the darkness. You will understand how this technique helps protect young birds from the dangers of becoming prey to some raptor looking for a tasty lunch.

If you listen to its calls, you will quickly discover where it obtained its name. Jackdaw's most common sounds are its contact calls - the sound it uses to keep in touch with other family members - which sounds like 'jack, jack, jack'. However, when it wants to warn other birds of approaching danger, it gives a close impression of the rook with a deeper sounding 'daw'.

Jackdaws prefer to nest in the protection of a hollow tree, the cleft in a rock or on the ground in abandoned rabbit burrows. The nest is nothing special; however, the lining can be interesting as they try to make it cosy. I have watched fascinated as a pair of jackdaws plucked the hair from cattle residing in the field next to our home. The cattle seemed oblivious to the jackdaws' constant attention as they landed on their backs and proceeded to pull tufts of hair from their bodies. Most of us use a comb, although I have little need for one these days, as most of my hair departed years ago. A comb removes loose hair and tidies up what remains. Cattle and sheep cannot comb themselves, so the jackdaw lends a helping hand or, more correctly, beak. It removes loose hair and picks off ticks, mites, and other parasites, providing a win-win situation for cattle and birds.

Another interesting fact about the jackdaw is that it is one of our most intelligent birds. Tests have shown that it can solve simple puzzles to obtain food and even count to uncover hidden treats.

ROOK

The rook is larger than the jackdaw and has an enormous grey proboscis. Okay, I know that is not the correct word. I just threw it in to be clever! All budding ornithologists and naturalists understand that a 'proboscis' is a mammal's elongated nose, not a bird's beak.

However, the rook is the only corvid with an enormous grey beak, making it relatively straightforward to identify. We have rooks visiting the garden, for which I am glad, as they usually waddle around the base of my bird table, assisting the pigeons and doves in picking up seeds dropped by other birds. They are also common in town and city centres, or somewhere some careless person might drop a little free food.

At one time, we considered purchasing a house in a fantastic location with a 'rookery' in the trees alongside the garden. The house was close to a coastal path where we regularly walk the dogs. I have seen this rookery in all its guises through the year. Spring though is exceptional with the noise of the rooks' constant sounds from the multitude of nests, some only metres apart; it certainly was a place to stop and listen. The calls and heckles of so many birds would cause the hair on the back of your head to stand on end. It is an incredible experience.

Rooks are social birds nesting together in large numbers. They also tend to be early risers, and I often wonder if we had purchased the house whether we would have survived the days of spring when the young were in the nest, and the 'cawing' of the parent birds would be at its loudest.

CARRION CROW AND HOODED CROW

These are perhaps the most common of all the corvid family. The carrion crow is found mainly in England and now spreading north into Scotland. The hooded is a bird of the west and located along the western fringes of Scotland and throughout Ireland. These two birds are so closely related they are usually placed together in bird guides and other publications.

Crows are neat birds with delightfully curved upper beaks and round heads. They are opportunistic hunters, enjoying nothing more than robbing the eggs from the nests of other birds. Egg 'dumps' have been discovered in many locations where the crows have left the remnants of their various meals.

Amazingly, crows can fish similarly to the eagle, pulling fish out of the water's surface. They can also copy the peregrine's hunting prowess and drop out of the sky onto unsuspecting prey.

Anyone living around the coast may have discovered 'crows cups' along the beach. These are empty shellfish shells that crows have dropped from a height onto rocks below to break them open. They then swoop down to eat the contents.

I remember staying at a friend's house several years ago and looking out with delight into the garden to see a hooded crow.

"Wow!" I exclaimed to my bemused friend, "A hoodie!"

"What's so special about that old crow?" he countered, baffled at my excitement.

"I don't see them very often," I explained, "they are quite rare where we live."

"Please feel free to take a few hundred home with you; they are nothing but a noisy nuisance to me, digging up my lawn and flower borders."

My friend's comments are typical of perhaps most people who see these birds as nothing more than pests that should be destroyed before they destroy the things we like.

RAVEN

I am always thrilled to catch sight of a raven. Thankfully, on one of our clifftop walks, we are fortunate enough to see ravens quite frequently, and they are awe-inspiring birds. Perhaps I enjoy seeing them because they are scarce around our island, only numbering just over four thousand pairs.

The easiest way to recognise the raven is by size. They are similar to a buzzard. The beak is large and black, with a fine feathered covering extending halfway along the upper mandible. Also, look at the neck and chin area; the raven has a prominent beard observed when the bird is sitting. The last thing required to make a positive observation is when flying, each of its impressive wings ends with long, loose finger-like feathers.

During the Victorian era, ravens were considered good pets among the elite, with the author Charles Dickens owning two birds. A small flock of ravens have been kept at the Tower of London for several hundred years. According to records, they were present at the executions of Anne Boleyn (1536) and Lady Jane Grey (1554). It has been suggested that the birds were introduced to bring a foreboding or fear to the primary place of executions in medieval times. A legend states that if the raven ever leaves the Tower of London, Great Britain will fall soon afterwards.

Ravens are God's bin collectors, feeding predominantly off carrion (dead animals and birds). They often pick a carcass clean of all its flesh, similar to vultures. Ravens are the largest of our perching birds and are well able to kill for their dinner and will even tackle a snarling stoat or a curled-up hedgehog if required. It can be a rather fearsome bird.

CHOUGH

The first time you see a chough, you will take a second look as you ponder whether it is a carrion crow, jackdaw or rook that you are observing. Then you will notice its distinctive red bill and legs, hear its clear 'chuff, chuff, chuff' call, and be chuffed to bits at your discovery! There are only about one thousand two hundred pairs currently breeding in Britain and Ireland; therefore, you will have seen a rare and remarkable bird.

Once common around the coastline, choughs collapsed in numbers during the eighteen hundreds. Today, small clusters can be found in Cornwall and some of Scotland's Outer Hebridean islands. The most significant population can be found along Ireland's spectacular west coast.

I know some nest on high cliffs only twenty miles from my home; however, I enjoyed my best encounters with these unusual corvids in Jersey.

I have often discovered that if my camera is pointed in a particular direction with the zoom fully extended, someone will stop and look towards where the camera is trained. It happened on this occasion.

"What's he doing," a young lad asked his dad as they walked past.

"Taking a photo."

"What of?"

"I don't know. Perhaps the view?"

Anyone who knows the Grosnez headland in Jersey knows it would not be the best place to take 'view' photos. It's a pleasant enough place with a delightful old ruined fort. The fact that I was not looking in the direction of the ruin but aiming toward the ground made his comment all the stranger.

"What are you photographing?" The curious youngster asked, leaving his father's side and approaching me.

"Choughs," I replied, pointing out the unusual black birds a short distance away.

"Crows," the boy's father responded incredulously.

"No, choughs," I replied with the authority of an avian expert.

"Pardon," the father replied.

"These are choughs," I repeated, "a member of the corvid family."

The father smiled, "Crows, they are crows."

I felt like giving up at this point but persevered. "They might look like crows, but they are far less common; in fact, they are quite rare and called choughs," I explained. "There are seven corvid family members in the UK; five are black, and two are more colourful. The crow is also a corvid, as are magpies and jays, but this is the rarest of them all, and it is a chough."

"Oh!" the father said in surprise, "really?"

"Yes, it's a chough. See the red beak and legs, that's how you know it's a chough. It's the only corvid with a red beak."

"Oh!" the father repeated, "really?"

Father and son were moved back toward mother and a little sister who had remained aloof during the inquisition.

"Happy picture taking," he concluded as he gave a half-wave.

As they walked away, I heard the son ask, "Dad, what was that man talking about?"

There was a slight pause before the faint answer came back that I was not supposed to hear, "I haven't a clue, and I don't think he knew either!"

MAGPIE

The black and white magpie is such a common bird that most of us do not give it a second glance when it visits our gardens. As with many other species considered in this book, do stop and take a closer examination. The black colouring is blue and a wonderfully iridescent blue at that. Now look along the wing and notice the added green hues. There is more to the magpie than first meets the eye.

When I was young, I learnt a little ditty about the magpie:-

One for sorrow, Two for joy,
Three for a girl, Four for a boy,
Five for silver, Six for gold,
Seven for a secret never to be told
Eight for a dream, Nine for a wish,
Ten is a bird that you must not miss.

As a boy, my father told me stories about magpies taking anything shiny they saw. My grandparents would close windows if they saw one in the vicinity of their house in case it was tempted to swoop inside, perform a dash and grab raid and make off with the family silver!

I have never personally witnessed a magpie stealing anything; however, I have seen the sad results. We have several nest boxes around our garden, two of which are homemade by hollowing a log using a chainsaw. The nesting chamber was quite deep, and, as I was limited in the size of drill bits, I made the entrance hole thirty-five millimetres wide instead of the recommended thirty-two millimetres for birds up to sparrow size.

I was delighted to see a pair of tree sparrows almost immediately take up residence, and shortly after, they began the daily routine of bringing food to a young brood. I watched them work busily for nearly a fortnight, and then one morning, I noticed three clumps of nesting material on the ground near the nest box. When I looked at the nesting site, I saw nesting material hanging out of the entrance. It was evident that something had raided the nest, pulled out the chick and possibly the parent bird, and devoured them on the lawn where the bits of nesting material had been left. The magpie that nested in a large tree alongside our home had been at work. The nest was ruined, the chicks killed, and the parents fled.

Magpies have also, in the past, used the same tricks as blue tits to steal cream from the tops of milk bottles. The thought of a magpie's beak that had recently been tearing into some dead creature on a roadside now dipping deeply into your daily milk delivery is enough to put you off milk for life.

Occasionally, in the milkman's days, magpies also learned how to open egg boxes left with the milk to steal the hen's eggs inside.

Perhaps the magpie's behaviour inspired the famous Italian composer Gioachino Rossini to write a renowned opera called 'The Thieving Magpie'.

JAY

A jay's visit to the garden adds an exciting splash of colour to any dull day, as does spotting one while walking in the woods. Although a member of the usually dull corvid family, the jay certainly knows how to turn on the image in style.

Its pink body, black and white wings and mottled blue covert feathers certainly catch your attention. As with many other birds we have considered in these pages, jays were persecuted during Victorian times, so their colourful feathers could be used in lady's hats and even for making flies for fishing.

On one occasion, I was on the phone chatting to someone when Karen came to my study door in some excitement. In silence, as if playing charades, she motioned that she needed my camera, which I passed to her as I chatted away.

After several unsuccessful attempts at acting out another task, I covered the receiver and asked, "What's the matter?"

"Jay!" she whispered, "In the garden; how do I take a photo?"

I quickly explained as she disappeared, camera in hand.

Despite all my best endeavours to cut the conversation short, the person on the other end of the line kept moving to another subject. It was infuriating. I attempted to change position in the hope of seeing the jay further up the garden by looking through the window at an acute angle. It didn't work.

Karen reappeared, camera in hand and showed me the pictures she had taken of the jay searching my lawn for grubs or buried acorns. Finally, the conversation ended, and I darted into the sunroom to see my prize visitor, only for my sudden appearance to startle the jay and for it to take flight. I was disappointed.

The next day Karen poked her head around the office door and said, "The jay's back," and so it was.

The brightly coloured bird visited daily for the next three weeks, allowing me to take impressive pictures as it hopped, jumped, pecked and dug in various areas of my lawn. Then, just when I had visions of it nesting nearby, it was gone, never to return. The visit was a short special time when a usually retiring bird graced my garden.

I hope you will now look out for the seven corvids of Great Britain and Ireland and see each of these rather exciting birds in a slightly different light than just saying, "Oh! There's another crow!"

When our daughter was young, we purchased a cassette tape (yes, that long ago) called 'Creation Songs' recorded by Buddy Davis. Many of the tunes and words were very good; however, one stood out in my mind. It was called 'The Seven C's of History', and it went like this:

I have committed to my memory
Important events from the Scriptures I read
With music we'll learn, a song is the key
To remember the seven C's of History

Creation, Corruption, Catastrophe,
Confusion, Christ and the Cross,
Consummation it is the last C
The Seven C's of History

There's no rhyme or reason why we can't comprehend
Histories events from beginning to end
It would be an adventure. I know you'll agree
To remember the seven C's of history

The Bible's the history of the universe
I'll stand on its promise, Believe every verse
We cleared the ground. Let's scatter the seed
Our faith is based in real history

Perhaps you need to listen to the song to learn those seven C's. However, they provide a concise and straightforward guide to Bible history. Let us interpret them.

- **Creation** – of all things by God - Genesis chapter 1
- **Corruption** – Adam and Eve disobey God and sin - Genesis chapter 3
- **Catastrophe** – Noah and the great flood - Genesis chapters 6 to 9
- **Confusion** – the tower of Babel and confusion of languages - Genesis chapter 11
- **Christ** – the four Gospels detailing the life and work of the Lord Jesus - Matthew, Mark, Luke and John
- **Cross** – the death of Christ – Matthew chapter 27, Mark chapter 15, Luke chapter 23 and John chapter 19
- **Consummation** – the coming again of the Lord Jesus and future events - Revelation.

As the song says, committing to memory important things from the Bible is good. How about trying to learn a verse a week? I now regret that I never spent longer memorising Bible texts when I was younger. Don't miss out. Start today.

I will delight myself in Thy statutes:
I will not forget Thy Word.
(Psalm 119 v16)

FANTASTIC MR FOX

Fascinating Facts
Foxes are the only members of the dog family that can retract their claws like cats. North American grey foxes are the only dogs that can climb trees. A foxes den is called an 'earth', which is suitable because the cubs are born black, blind, and deaf onto bare earth with no added nesting material. Although foxes can live up to ten years, mortality rates are high, with only 1 in 50 foxes living beyond five years.

I clearly remember where and when I first saw a wild fox. I was visiting a building site with my father, where he was overseeing the development of new houses in Baildon, West Yorkshire. I was eight years old.

We left the working area, as I wanted to explore a wooded valley at the rear of some of the gardens. In those days, such a place appealed to me, not so much as somewhere to see wildlife but, as a 'wannabe' police detective, somewhere that a criminal might hide his loot. I might just end up uncovering a murder mystery. I didn't!

My father and I cautiously walked down the steep incline towards the bottom through a mature forest of oak, beech, and the occasional sycamore tree. He pointed out the different leaf shapes of the various species. For the most part, I was looking for any signs of buried treasure. In my mind, I was not with my father; we were both detectives searching for a possible crime scene.

Eventually, we turned and headed back up the hill towards the various men and machinery working on the building site above us. As we neared the top, I looked back, hoping to unravel some mystery! Instead, I saw a red dog trotting lightly along the path through the bottom of the valley. I looked towards the direction from which it had come but could see no owner. Suddenly my brain kicked into gear, and I realised what it was – a fox!

"Dad, there's a fox," I called out rather too loudly and excitedly.

My father turned around while the fox stopped and looked up to see what had made all the noise. For a few seconds, father and excited son gazed down at the beautiful red fox while it stared back at us. Then it sped away, disappearing down the track, long bushy tail trailing behind. I felt goosebumps rise across my body and the hairs on my neck stood on end in excitement. It was almost as if I was filled with static electricity.

"A fox," my father said after it had gone, "not often, you see one of those in broad daylight."

It was my first time in either night or day, and a moment I will never forget. I spoke about the brief encounter so often, wondering how and where I could come across more foxes, that my parents bought me a book called 'Mammals, Tracks Trails and Signs' for my birthday. I read the book and traced its illustrations repeatedly, looking at footprints, fur deposits and other less savoury signs of animal visitation. I became a detective, but one tracking wildlife, not criminals.

Over the years, I have seen foxes on many occasions, usually early in the morning, as they make their way back to their den after a night's hunting. As I have learned more about this majestic and widespread but often elusive animal, I have marvelled at the extraordinary abilities of the red fox.

I was surprised to discover that the female only becomes fertile (able to have cubs) three days a year and only between December and

January. If she does not mate within that three-day window, she will not be able to raise a family for another year.

On one occasion, we were travelling through Bedfordshire when I saw three foxes playing together in a field. I safely pulled the car over to the side to observe their antics. It soon became apparent that there was one vixen (female) and two dogs (males). Both males were looking for the same female and chased each other around the field, barking, snapping and fighting for mating rights.

Although the foxes were away across the field, it was evident which the dominant fox was. I had a limited zoom camera in those days, and even with my best efforts, the pictures taken were distant, grainy, and despite leaning on a post, showing distinct signs of camera shake. Still, it was another never to be forgotten moment.

Most foxes seen during the day will be either old or sickly and usually unable to obtain the food they require at night because they are not as quick and agile as younger, fitter animals. You can generally tell if the fox is young or old by looking at its fur. Like humans, older foxes will be going grey around the head and along the flanks and tail. Younger animals will be a much sharper red all over.

I once saw a fox foraging around in a field as I headed out for lunch one Sunday with friends after attending the Sunday morning meeting in their local church.

"It's an old fox," I explained, noticing the grey was very prominent across its body as it buried its snout into the ground, looking for grubs and worms.

Two hours later, heading back to where I was staying, I looked into the field again and was surprised to see the fox still there. I stopped the car and, opening the passenger window, started taking photos. The old fox seemed oblivious to my presence as it scratched for any tiny morsel it could find in its hunger.

I tried to imagine the tired old fox in its prime, vivid red, a thick bushy tail, and clean white underparts. Was this once a proud dominant dog that had lost its position in the hierarchy of the animal world? Had it been beaten and chased by a fitter, stronger, brighter young upstart? I would have loved to have known the history of this lone, hungry fox. Nature is like that; the more we discover, the more we want to know and the less we realise we do know. Such are the wonders of God's unfathomable creation.

Several years ago, I had a week of children's meetings in London. We were together as a family, and to avoid burdening anyone with looking after us, we had borrowed my parents-in-law's caravan for the week and stayed on a pleasant site just outside Croydon.

One evening as dusk descended, I was stretched out on the seating area reading when a movement outside the caravan window caught my eye. I looked into the gloom to see a fox rummaging in the grass about five metres away. I silently signalled to the family as I cautiously got up and pulled my camera from the overhead locker. I then proceeded to open the window quietly. The fox did not seem to notice my presence as I poked my camera through the open window and tried to take a couple of photos.

As it moved away, I wondered if I might be able to follow it. I jumped out of the caravan and shadowed the fox at a safe distance. Other people on the site also spotted the fox as it wove between caravans, cars and awnings. Someone threw down a chicken leg which the fox jumped on and gobbled with delight. The lady who threw it gingerly offered another, holding it at arm's length. The fox approached cautiously, watched by six or seven onlookers, and took the leg before scampering away.

It was indeed a close encounter of the thrilling kind; to be so near to a wild fox as to almost be able to stroke it, it certainly made that visit to London extra special.

It was on another visit to England's capital that, once again, I was captivated at the sight and shenanigans of these beautiful creatures.

I had flown in to speak at a Christian conference in Tooting. As my hosts parked outside their house, I was astonished to see a fox strolling along the pavement towards us. It seemed to be without a care in the world.

"There's a fox," I exclaimed in astonishment.

"It's an urban fox," my host responded, "if you look out of your window tonight without the light on, you will see several."

The evening seemed to drag as I waited for dark and the excitement of watching the nocturnal adventures of London's suburban foxes.

When I finally went to my room, I made myself comfortable and sat in the window, looking up the road leading to the house. I did not have long to wait as a fox soon strode with purposeful steps into sight, jumped over a wall and into someone's front garden.

Another appeared from a different direction, and within no time, I was trying to keep track of five other foxes as they ran, jumped and trotted around the houses and through the gardens down the road. One disappeared behind a car only to suddenly reappear, standing proudly on the vehicle's roof. I recalled that I had once parked on a street in London and discovered footprints over my car the following morning. I had thought they belonged to a cat; I suddenly realised a fox had probably left them.

The fox stood on the car roof for about half a minute, surveying its relatives as they continued their search for food in and out of various gardens. It then jumped lightly onto the bonnet and then down onto the road. Someone opening a door further along the street caused a temporary scattering of the foxes to some undergrowth, only to continue their fun and games once they knew the coast was clear and safe. One managed to obtain a plastic bag and ran along the road with its prized haul, frantically pursued by three others trying to lend a hand... paw! It was the highest quality of entertainment I could ever wish to see.

After a good hour and a half's worth of theatricals, I was left with the occasional appearances of only two foxes and realised it was time to draw the curtains and get into bed. My only disappointment as I drifted happily off to sleep that night was that I would be returning home the next day, so I would not have another night to delve into the nocturnal world of Mr and Mrs Fox.

The Bible does not put the fox in a very favourable light. King Herod is called 'that fox' by the Lord Jesus. The Lord was speaking about Herod's cunning, sly fox-like character.

Song of Solomon in the Bible is not an easy book to understand, even for the most knowledgeable of Christians. There is, however, a short verse that speaks about foxes.

Take us the foxes, the little foxes, that spoil the vines: for our vines have tender grapes.
(Song of Solomon Ch2 v15)

The cubs, little foxes, would attack the vines upon which the tender grapes grew. The grapes were an essential source of food and drink to the people in Bible times. Grapes also speak of joy. If the vine died, the grapes could not be harvested, and the people would grow hungry and lose their joy of living.

The little foxes are a picture of sin. Maybe its just fear, jealousy, pride an unkind tongue. These sins ruin things such as courage, love, generosity and honesty. They creep in slowly but dangerously, and once they are allowed to dominate our lives, they rob us of the joy of being saved.

Therefore we need to look out for the little foxes of sin to ensure they do not take from us the enjoyment of salvation in the Lord Jesus.

DIFFERENT DUCKS
– QUACKING, DABBLING BIRDS

Jemima her story is told in the introduction

Fascinating Facts
The saying 'like water off a duck's back' is true; the outer feathers of a duck are so waterproof that even when diving its warmer downy feathers underneath never get wet. Ducks are omnivorous, meaning they eat various things, from plants to insects to fruit and fish.

Ducks are unique birds. There are diving ducks like the goldeneye and tufted duck and dabbling ducks such as the common mallard or the massive billed shoveler. Then there are the rather elegant or striking-looking ducks such as the teal, pintail or the pretty little mandarin. Ducks come in all shapes, sizes, colours, types, and seasons. If we add the two specialist sawbills, the goosander and the red-breasted merganser, we suddenly have a whole flock of swimming, flying, dabbling, diving, and exciting birds. They are a birdwatcher's dream, and because they tend to be larger, most can be seen by the naked eye without costly binoculars or telescopes.

Goosander

I remember the enjoyment as a very young boy of being taken by my mother to some local park with a stale loaf of bread to feed the ducks. At four years old, I had no idea that bread was not good for ducks or any birds because it swelled in their stomachs.

We have a unique photo of our daughter, aged about three, standing on a stone mounting block surrounded by hungry ducks she had been feeding with grain, not bread. There were so many dabbling around her wellies that I am convinced she thought she might be on their list of yummy fare.

At some time or other, most of us have fed the ducks. We have discovered how confident they can be as they waddle around our feet, seeking to gobble up any food items we have dropped. They are engaging birds, especially the familiar mallard.

Just stop next time you see a mallard, look closely at that beautiful green head on the male bird, it is rather impressive, then wait a bit, and look again and you will wonder whether it is green or a sort of navy blue or perhaps more a purply blue colour?

Certain bird feathers are like that; they can appear to change colour as they refract the light. Think about starlings and crows; look at cormorants and shags, then the magpie and kingfisher. They all have feathers that can appear black, brown, blue or green, depending on the light. Who else but God could create something as unique as that?

Pintail

It is always worth looking at ducks because you never know what you might find. The tufted duck, for instance - is it a tufty, or could it be the less common goldeneye? Have a second glance at that female mallard; is it a mallard, or perhaps a garganey? Watching and spotting ducks can be great fun.

Shortly after we knew we would purchase our new home, we took our daughter to show her the partially built house. Having tried to explain in the bare breeze block shell of the house what was what and what would be where we headed back home the longer but more scenic way. As we rounded a bend that led onto a longish straight bit of road, starting to cross in front of us was a mother duck with nine young ducklings. I anchored on the brakes and stopped to let the family cross the road. I put on my hazard warning lights to alert cars behind to the danger. The two cars following me stopped as they could just see past me to the duck family, slowly waddling after their mother across the busy road. It was a gloriously happy sight with the 'WOW' factor.

My attention was suddenly drawn to a silver car approaching from the opposite direction. It had a much clearer view than I had of the little family shuffling across the road, yet the vehicle did not seem to be slowing down. I frantically started to flash my lights to warn him. In my mad panic, I forgot about the horn as I attempted to get my window open to wave my hand.

The car rushed on with no attempt to slow down; then, the baby ducklings disappeared in a cloud of feathers underneath the rushing vehicle. The mother duck and the leading three ducklings were clear and ran in panic across the grass verge and into the safety of the hedgerow. As the car passed, utter carnage was left in its wake. Five dead, mangled ducklings were thrown about in the road. One poor little thing was on its side, flapping its little wing in obvious distress. I leapt out of the car, feeling very angry, while our daughter in the back of the car asked, "How could they do that?" It was a good question that I have still never been able to answer.

Tufted Duck

I picked up the injured trembling bird and held it tenderly in my hands, its blood dampening my fingers. I passed it to my daughter, "You hold this one while I move the dead ones off the road."

As my daughter exited the car, the little creature gave one last flap of distress and went limp, joining its siblings as victims of a seemingly callous and uncaring driver. Further up the road, the car that had caused such carnage stopped and then quickly sped off. The Bible instructs us to *'be angry and sin not,'* however, at that point, I was glad the driver was far enough away from me so that I was angry but did not sin. The driver in the car behind had also got out, "That man must have seen them," he said, "you were blocking this side of the road... he should have slowed down."

"I even flashed my lights at him," I explained exasperatedly.

Like us, he was devastated at the carnage of ducklings lying on the road.

I picked up the six mangled ducklings and gently lay them next to each other on the grass verge along the side of the road, my hands stained red with the blood. Devastated, we continued the journey home.

Later that evening, I went back to the scene and, picking up the broken bodies, took them to the garden of what was to be our new home, where I buried them.

All week I brooded about what we had seen. I looked up the address of the local newspaper's letters page and wrote an email to them describing the whole incident. I never expected that it would be published, but it was in print in the paper two weeks later. I realised I could have worded it slightly better as I read it. One or two Christians contacted me to sympathise. I just hoped the driver who killed the ducks read it and maybe had some feeling of guilt.

Several years later, Karen came home to tell me that three relatively large ducklings had been lying dead on the same road but closer to our home. Our daughter had got out and moved them off the road, but one mangled victim she was unable to lift. I set off in the car, donned my gloves picked up the three nearly full-sized ducklings and brought them home to bury. Once again, I questioned how any driver could fail to see or avoid such sizeable birds. It felt that their lives were wasted. They had started well, been cared for by the mother bird and were nearly ready to leave her protection and take flight, only for their lives to be cut tragically short.

Very sadly, some young Christians end up similarly. Their life of Christian usefulness is cut short. It could be that like a man in the Bible called Demas, they love the things of the world too much and end up living as though they had never been saved. Others may be tempted into some sad sin that damages their testimony and stunts their Christian growth. The important thing is to daily read the Bible, pray and keep close to God. The apostle Paul encourages us:

This I say then, walk in the Spirit, and ye shall not fulfil the lust of the flesh. For the flesh lusteth against the Spirit, and the Spirit against the flesh: and these are contrary the one to the other: so that ye cannot do the things that ye would. And they that are Christ's have crucified the flesh with the affections and lusts. If we live in the Spirit, let us also walk in the Spirit.

(Galatians Ch5 v16-17 & 24)

To crucify the flesh and live in the Spirit means to forsake our own will and desires and walk according to God's will and follow His plan for our lives.

Shovler

Wigeon

COMPELLING CORMORANTS AND SHINY SHAGS
– BIG BLACK BEAUTIES

Cormorant

Fascinating Facts
Cormorants can fly at up to 35 miles per hour and dive to 45 metres staying underwater for up to four minutes. It is a member of the pelican family and can eat 1 kilogram of fish a day. Shags have a green shine when seen in direct sunlight, which gives it the name of the 'green cormorant.' Shags are more abundant than cormorants outnumbering their larger counterparts by four or five to one.

If you visit any coastal location, you will invariably see some large black-looking birds perched on rocks or swimming and diving in the sea. These are either cormorants or the smaller shag, and it takes a little while to sort them out.

If you see a large black bird with a long yellow beak on an inland lake, reservoir or river, you can be sure it is a cormorant. Shags are saltwater birds only and never venture inland to freshwater, as do cormorants.

Shag

The shag is smaller, neater and greener, without any white on its face. You may well also see a lovely crest sitting on its head. The cormorant, however, tends to look blacker and more unkempt. Both are excellent swimmers, often braving the incoming breakers of a stormy sea and diving under the waves as they crash over them.

Fishermen generally hate cormorants because of their habit of coming inland to catch fish - their fish; fish that have often been bred for the angling community. As a result of such behaviour, cormorants have gained the nickname 'sea crows' to link them to the land scavenging corvids.

Cormorants often sit on a rock or post, holding their wings open to dry. They do this after they have been diving, fishing and eating. Hundreds of years ago, people looking at this practice decided it was a sign of an ill omen resulting in the cormorant being linked with dying and given the nickname 'black death'.

Those of you, eagle-eyed and into that rough game of football, may well think that this posture of the bird holding its wings out to dry looks familiar. The liver bird, much loved in Liverpool and used as a symbol on the football team's jersey, is based on a cormorant striking this pose.

Sitting in a bird hide overlooking a large expanse of water one summer day, I considered moving on as nothing too exciting seemed to be showing up. I had enjoyed my fill of mallards, shovelers, coots, moorhens and herons when in the distance, I caught sight, through my binoculars, of a cormorant swimming on the water's surface. It suddenly dived and seconds later reappeared, holding a giant eel in its beak. A cormorant is a little less than a metre in length, and the eel seemed equally as long as it wriggled and squirmed, attempting to free itself from the cormorant's grasp. The eel was gripped, and I was gripped. The fight was quite far away; however, I turned my camera on and, using the maximum zoom, commenced photographing this life-or-death struggle.

Cormorant and Eel

The eel threw itself around the neck of the cormorant, and both dived beneath the water. I was sure the eel would have the upper hand here, in its natural element. The two combatants emerged from the depths, still locked in their death tussle. The eel wrapped its body around the cormorant's beak, still holding it fast. Once again, it threw itself snake-like around the bird's neck, and as it seemed to contract, I expected the cormorant to release its grip. It didn't.

Down they both went again under the water. When they emerged, the eel had released itself from the neck of the large black bird and was futilely thrashing about in the air. Meanwhile, the cormorant commenced slapping the unfortunate eel on the water's surface, obviously in the hope of stunning it.

The battle lasted about five minutes as bird and fish each sought supremacy over the other. With supreme skill and great patience, the cormorant gradually positioned the eel so that it could commence swallowing it headfirst. I was engrossed and suddenly realised that I had stopped taking photos. As I resumed the clicking, the eel started to disappear, still wriggling and writhing, into the gullet of the cormorant. It was quite a sight as the big bird strained to swallow its colossal catch. Slowly, the eel's length, still threshing about, shortened as more and more disappeared into the cavernous stomach of the hungry bird. Finally, only about four inches of the eel's tail remained, and no matter how hard the cormorant attempted to swallow, flap its wings or stretch its neck, it was evident that it was so full it could not fit the rest of the eel inside!

Cormorant having swallowed the Eel

The cormorant sat very low in the water due to the eel's weight, with the fish's tail visible out of its mouth. It must have been a very uncomfortable experience, and I wondered, as I watched the neck of the bird sticking out of the water, how long it would be before the bird could fly again?

Shags are the much-underrated cousins of the cormorant and can often look almost prehistoric as they stretch their long necks or flash their distinctively green eyes. The eyes are more than distinctive; they can look positively evil as they catch the sun's rays.

If you get the opportunity, watch both as they dive for fish from a swimming position. The cormorant plunges below the water in a most ungainly manner. The shag, on the other hand, gives a little jump out of the water before disappearing with little more than a ripple. It is almost as if it is showing off in some Olympic diving competition and saying, 'look at me, I'm a gold medal diver!'

These two birds are always seen by water, as they dive down to obtain the food they require. Ezekiel, a prophet of the Lord, wrote a rather large book in the Old Testament. He tells us how God allowed him to see certain future events. In one, he saw a river.

He brought me through the waters;
the waters were to the ankles.
He brought me through the waters;
the waters were to the knees.
He brought me through; the waters were to the loins.
It was a river that I could not pass over:
for the waters were risen, waters to swim in,
a river that could not be passed over.
(Ezekiel Ch47 v3-6)

Ezekiel saw the waters rising until they were so deep he could swim in them. The Bible is like that. We begin our Christian life enjoying the beautiful Bible stories. Then we learn some of the more challenging things in the lives of the great men and women of faith until we progress to where we are swimming in the great truths of the Bible and learning to depend upon God more. We discover by reading and studying the Bible that no matter who we are, we can never exhaust the depths of the wisdom of God as revealed in Holy Scripture. The Bible is a book to swim in!

REMARKABLE ROBINS
– THE GARDENER'S FRIEND

Fascinating Facts
Young robins practice singing quietly through Autumn and Winter in readiness for spring when they want to be in tune and harmony to attract a mate. On 15th December 1960, the robin was declared Britain's national bird. Only one in four birds will live beyond their first birthday.

My father owned a stainless steel spade with a beautiful wooden shaft and a comfortable D-shaped handle. It must have been purchased around the time of my birth. Due to the spade's construction and quality, I guess it was costly when my dad bought it. I am delighted to have the spade in my possession still, and even though the shaft is cracked and unable to undertake heavy work, I have no desire to fix it. It has too many memories of my father attached to it.

One of those memories involved a robin. It was the summer of 1976, which was incredibly hot. My father's thermometer attached to the outside of the shed, catching the sun, stayed in the high nineties (about 35 degrees celsius) day after day. It was roasting.

Most evenings, when the temperature cooled, my dad would head out into the garden to potter about doing odd jobs such as hoeing, weeding and generally trying to keep the garden looking good. Each time he took his trusty spade and would place it into the soil close to where he was working.

I clearly remember when my father came to the dining room door to get my attention. His spade stood at the bottom of the garden, and a robin was sitting on top of the handle. It remained contentedly in place as we crept down the path to look closer. Then it burst into a loud hearty song as if to say, 'I'm happy, but please don't come any closer and crowd my space!'

The little robin regularly returned to perch on my father's spade handle in the cooler evenings throughout that long hot summer. Sometimes it would sing; occasionally, it would dart off the spade onto the ground to catch some juicy bug. Mostly it remained, seemingly contented, sitting and watching my father at work.

To my mother and I, it appeared to be overseeing dad's labours to ensure that what he was doing, he was doing well. The robin was the foreman and my father the labourer, it seemed as if when it approved of my father's efforts, it sang, and if it didn't, it remained quiet!

Many can testify to the robin's tameness, some even managing to get them to eat out of their hands.

When I visit schools to conduct one of my 'bird talks', I always attempt to involve the children. As I display pictures of different birds, I ask if anyone knows what they are.

Showing a chaffinch photo, I ask "Does anyone know which bird this is?"

"Robin!" comes the enthusiastic answer.

Then a bullfinch photo – "Anyone know this bird?"

"Robin!" again spoken with vigour by the child answering.

I sigh deeply but press on with a picture of a house sparrow.

"You must know this bird?"

"Robin!" The third attempt from a child with maybe some hesitation.

Surprisingly that little scenario is relatively common. The only bird many children have ever heard of is the robin, yet they seem to have little idea of how to recognise one.

During the colder, darker winter months, most birds remain silent, perhaps to help conserve vital energy required to keep warm. The robin is different and will still sing his loud hearty song from the top of a leafless bush when the frost lies on the ground.

The robin also sings at night. I have gone outside on several occasions near midnight and heard a bird singing loudly. This song pattern has been documented over the centuries. The robin is usually the first bird to sing in the 'dawn chorus'. This remarkable bird symphony reaches its melodious peak in May when at first light, bird after bird starts to sing until a whole woodland appears to be alive and ringing with birdsong. The entire chorus needs to be experienced to appreciate how incredible it is.

Robins are very territorial. Once they set up a nest in an area, they do not tolerate other robins venturing into their 'patch'. I have observed this behaviour in several gardens. Two male birds postulate with raised tails, head down, feathers fluffed, chest puffed out, and wings held slightly apart, looking bigger and more intimidating to the rival bird. I have seen them fighting too. A flurry of wings, beaks and legs seemingly in a tangle as they lift a couple of feet off the ground.

I have never observed a vicious encounter such as this ending in death, even though such events are sadly relatively common.

While walking the dogs close to home, Wellington, one of our Cavalier King Charles spaniels, dived into the hedgerow, as he often did, mooched around and then rejoined the path along which we were walking. Another twenty metres later, I saw him walking just behind me, head held proudly in the air and the body of a dead robin in his mouth.

Somehow, we have failed to teach any of our dogs to 'give' on command, and they see us trying to get something from them as a jolly game involving them ducking, diving and running, making us look totally stupid. Eventually, Wellington came within catching distance, and a quick grab of the collar ended his little game.

The dead robin he had been carrying looked in perfect condition, except for dog saliva. Had it been hit by a car, or was it perhaps a victim of its own kind? Had it fought and lost? We will never know.

Most birds are fussy about where they nest. The entrance hole must be the correct size, and the nest box must face the right direction. They also consider other important factors before moving into the upmarket accommodation we often provide for them.

The robin is not so fussy, but it does like an open-fronted nest box. To be novel, attach an empty clay plant pot securely on its side to a sheltered wall of the house or fence and see what happens. You could also put out an old teapot and screw it on its side, to something firm about three metres high. Robins tend to like this more quirky type of accommodation.

Robin following a fight

I have a recording of 'Hymns and Sacred Songs' recorded by a singer named Cowboy Copas. Sadly he is probably best known for dying in a plane crash that killed two other singers and his son-in-law, who was piloting the plane.

On this recording were several more unusual songs that I trust were evidence that he knew the Lord Jesus as his Saviour, and I do hope this was the case. One of those songs was called 'The Legend of the Robin Redbreast', a fictitious song from folklore suggesting that the robin obtained its red breast from its encounter with the Lord Jesus on the cross.

Oh, have you heard this story? It happened long ago
When Christ our blessed Saviour was here on earth below
An echo through the ages from distant Calvary
I'll tell it to you simply as it was told to me

It breathes the blessed teaching of God's own holy word
A lesson taught in meekness by a lowly little bird

When Jesus hung in sorrow, our debt of shame to pay
No one was there to comfort or wipe His tears away
A little bird flew near Him in sober coat of brown
And gazed in tender pity, then slowly fluttered down

With gentle wings, it fanned Him to cool His aching head
And hovered near His bosom, all stained with deepest red
At last, when all was ended, as if to mourn his loss
It rose with blood-stained feathers and circled around the cross

It flew away in sadness, and to this day, tis said
It wears upon its bosom that stain of crimson red
When I shall cross the valley and go to seek my rest
May I wear like the robin God's sign upon my breast

Although the parts about the little robin are just fictitious (made up), the song does remind us of the pain and loneliness the Lord Jesus suffered as He hung upon the cross where He was dying because of our sin.

Here is a verse from the Bible that you will hopefully remember every time you see a robin.

The blood of Jesus Christ His Son cleanseth us from all sin.
(1 John Ch1 v7)

DELIGHTFUL DEER
– DELICATE AND DEXTROUS

Red Deer

Fascinating Facts
Male deer are called Bucks or Stags, female deer are called Does, and young deer are called Fawns. All deer have a stomach with four chambers, and they can eat their food and then regurgitate it to give it another chew. It's a bit like being able to enjoy your favourite meal two or three days in a row. All male deer grow and cast their antlers each year. The Chinese Water deer lacks antlers but has tusks that look like fangs.

One thrill I have in holidaying in Scotland is the actual journey to wherever we are staying, usually in the Highlands. Once the car reaches Perth and commences driving north along the A9 trunk road, the majestic countryside never ceases to enthral me. Scotland is the land of kilts, bagpipes, haggis, heather, mountains and lochs, and it is also the land of the majestic red deer, the largest member of the deer family living in Britain and Ireland.

I often ask Karen to drive part of this stretch so I can scan the hillsides bordering the busy road for any sign of deer activity. I cannot remember when we have travelled this incredibly scenic journey without seeing deer at some point.

Red deer are not confined only to the beautiful Highlands of Scotland; large herds are found in the borders of Dumfries and Galloway and smaller numbers in various locations across England and Wales. The red deer can grow to nearly a metre and a half in size, excluding its head and antlers, so it should be easy to see.

Easy enough to see? Given its size, it should be! It is, after all, our largest wild mammal, excluding wild horses, but one of the incredible things about this most majestic-looking creature is how difficult it is to spot, even in its strongholds. It can keep well hidden in mature forests and only venture out at dusk when human danger is absent.

During one holiday along the Solway Firth, we enjoyed reading about the so-called Covenanters and visiting places connected with them. The story of this 17th century group of Christians who withstood the decree of kings who wanted to impose governmental rule on church meetings is the stuff of legends. Many of these brave men and women died for their faith in Christ! The area of Dumfries and Galloway, where we were staying, was a significant stronghold for this group, and stories in the area abound.

On one of our ventures out, we read about the opportunity to feed red deer in the company of a forest ranger. We required no further encouragement to go along the next day, and it just happened that this would be the last visitor trip to feed the deer that season. We arrived early to find several cars already in the car park, and by the time the ranger arrived toting two buckets of food, the place was bunged with people.

The sheer number of those attending to feed the red deer population was discouraging. My disappointment was not helped because the ranger told the assembled crowd that the usual number in attendance was ten and once he had twenty. As I looked around, I reckoned there were over one hundred on this occasion.

We walked in the crowd along a track that eventually led to a small wooden shed, beyond which was a tall wire 'deer fence'. These fences can be seen across the wilds of Scotland, where they are built to help contain the deer population and stop them from roaming into private gardens and across dangerous roads.

The ranger rattled the fence with his bucket, and suddenly, almost mysteriously, from out of the forest behind appeared one, then two, and a third deer. All walked, unfazed by the crowds, towards the food the ranger held out on the flat of his hand. Other deer joined them, and soon several magnificent red deer were grazing from his outstretched palm.

Once the invitation was given for others to participate in feeding, parents pushed, jostled, and cajoled themselves and their children into obtaining some of the precious feed. I held back a little, not wishing to push in front of others. I could see our daughter looking anxiously as the buckets quickly emptied, and I knew I had to use my six feet five and a half inches to get some food for her.

"Excuse me," I said as I attempted to reach a bucket.

It seemed that some of those around had never heard anyone using pleasantries as they grabbed handfuls of food at a time.

Finally, I squeezed past several onlookers and thrust my hand into the near-empty bucket. Thankfully my hands are in proportion to my body, allowing me to grasp a good amount to pass to our daughter, who was smiling delightedly at her father's brave attempts to get the food. She then made her way to the fence and, placing her hand holding the food through the mesh, was delighted when a huge stag meandered in her direction and gently took the feed from her. Thankfully, the ranger seeing his buckets rapidly emptying decided to open the wooden shed and bring out a bag full of a further supply of deer food. Our daughter obtained a second helping, this time without her father having to risk life and limb to get it. Once again, the big stag went for her hand as she stood beside the wire, grinning broadly. Despite the number of people, it was a day to remember.

On another occasion, I stayed in a house that had been kindly 'donated' for the week. I was conducting children's meetings in the nearby Gospel Hall and was delighted to have the peace and quiet of looking after myself during my visit.

While at this place, I discovered that a path along the banks of the River Thames was just three-quarters of a mile away, which I decided to walk each day. It was winter, and England was gripped by a strong Eastern airflow that brought heavy snow and reduced the daytime temperatures below freezing. I had not planned for such weather, and after suffering the discomfort of cold red hands the first day, I made a quick trip to the nearest town to purchase a pair of gloves.

The next day, gloves on, binoculars and camera around my neck, I set off to walk two miles upstream to a road bridge that crossed the river before returning along the same path. A marshy area to one side allowed me to obtain a glimpse or two of the elusive snipe if I bent down and peered through the vegetation.

The snipe is a long-billed bird that loves large expanses of soft ground into which it places its beak to feed. Snipe are notoriously tricky to see, hiding in the long grasses and reeds that grow in such muddy habitats. They can also remain incredibly still and only fly up with a sudden warning call and noisy flapping of wings when they feel you might stand on them. I was delighted, therefore, to obtain some relatively good views.

"Are you okay?" a gentleman asked as I straightened up. His sudden appearance made me nearly jump out of my skin. I had thought that at eight in the morning, with the temperature around minus six degrees, no one else would be foolish enough to have ventured out of the warmth of their homes.

Snipe

"Oh, yes, I am, thanks," I replied, trying to regain my composure.

"Good. I was a bit concerned as you seemed to be stuck. Bent right over as you were. I thought you'd done your back in or something."

"No, no. I was just looking for snipe."

"Pardon?"

"Snipe, I was looking for snipe."

"Oh, didn't know it grew around here."

"It's not a plant," I replied, "it's a bird."

"Not a plant? Snipe, did you say? Isn't it one of those herbs you put in food?"

"No, it is a long-billed bird, and there are three through the gap there right now."

"What for?"

"Pardon."

"What were you watching them for?"

"Because I'm a birdwatcher."

"Oh!" The gentleman seemed at a loss for words after that revelation.

"I see; well, enjoy yourself and watch your back bending over like that."

"I will," I laughed as he started on his way.

As I walked on, I wondered which of us was the dafter, him and his snipe plant or me and my birds!

A little further along the path, a sudden movement caught my eye. The bushes twenty-five metres in front of me were moving violently. As I watched, three roe deer suddenly sprung out and commenced running towards me. Instinctively I reached for my camera, knowing this was a once-in-a-lifetime moment.

Roe Deer

When the three deer were less than ten metres from me, they panicked as they sensed my presence for the first time. We stood looking at each other for a second before they turned and fled. Instead of dashing into the cover of the bushes from which they had appeared seconds earlier, they sprinted towards a large fence and stopped.

This unexpected turn of events allowed me the opportunity to take a couple of photos as they decided what to do. I was stunned when the leading deer took off from a standing position and jumped right over the fence to disappear into the undergrowth on the other side. The second deer required a little run before it launched itself over the fence to follow its companion out of sight at the other side.

The third deer was timid as it stood trembling and contemplating the fence. It suddenly came back towards me, then turned and ran full pelt toward the fence. I was sure it would jump over, but it seemed to chicken out at the last moment and veered off to its right. It spotted the bushes from which it had initially ventured and disappeared into the undergrowth.

The encounter left me exhilarated, having experienced a close brush with our most abundant deer species. Brilliant!

Muntjac Deer

The UK and Ireland boast six deer species, of which the smallest, the Reeves' muntjac deer, is the height of a medium-sized dog.

One morning on a memorable holiday to County Wicklow in Ireland, I got up early to go and see what birds were nearby, as early morning is often an excellent

Sika Deer

time to see some of the more uncommon species. As I stepped out of the house where we were staying and looked along the lane, a beautiful sika deer stood looking back at me.

As we looked at each other, fifty metres apart, I carefully unzipped my camera bag to remove my camera.

The deer stood still as if mildly amused at my efforts to get my camera in position. As I raised it to my eye and pressed the shutter to commence taking the pictures, I had visions of the deer bolting, leaving me with just a story to tell but no proof to offer. I took picture after picture as the deer stayed in place, occasionally moving round to show off its russet back and various whitish spots. It was almost as if it could read my mind allowing me to take pictures head-on and of both flanks. After a minute or so, it decided that I was no longer worth bothering with, and it turned and walked away, leaving me standing, camera in hand, counting my blessings for choosing to get out of bed early that morning.

Crowds and early mornings! I thought back to the people all wanting to feed the red deer in Scotland and how difficult it was to get an opportunity. I wondered how many people would have attended if the deer feeding time had been early in the morning when I saw the sika deer.

The morning is often the best time to get things done; at least, I find so. An important verse in the Bible states:

I love them that love me;
and those that seek me early shall find me.
(Proverbs Ch8 v17)

The best time of the day to read and pray is early in the morning, but not so early that you cannot stay awake. Many years ago, I decided to try getting up at five in the morning to be alone with God. The problem was that I had to walk around the house to read my Bible and pray because if I sat down, I would fall asleep.

It is good to give God the best part of the day before other things come in and crowd out your time spent with Him. I have often discovered, to my cost, that whenever I have had to put my quiet time with the Lord back to later in the day, so many other things crowded into my life, and it becomes increasingly hard to find those precious moments to be alone with God.

Start while you are young, cultivating a habit of seeking the Lord early. It will be something you will never regret.

Roe Deer

ACCIDENTS DO HAPPEN

– GREGARIOUS GEESE

When I was a junior engineer on an open cast coal mining site there happened to be an occasion when a part was required urgently in our workshop. The site manager, came into the engineer's office where we were all working.

"Right, an urgent job for one of you," he said, explaining that the needed part was in Leeds and was necessary to get our Dragline running. The Dragline was a colossal machine with a large bucket that could easily park a Land Rover inside with room to spare. We would sometimes do this when we showed groups of school children around the site. It was my party piece, even though it did stop production for a while.

"I'll go," I volunteered, thinking a trip into the city would be better than plotting survey readings any day.

"Okay, take my car; here's the address," said the site manager, handing me a piece of paper. "I believe the place is at the bottom of Scott Hall Road."

"Fine, I know that area well enough," I enthused, "I'll take the shortcut through the power station."

Russian White Fronted Goose

The shortcut was a trip I always enjoyed. You needed a security pass to travel through the power station, and we had one. It allowed us to save about five miles on a journey into Leeds city centre. Not only was it shorter, but it was far more exciting driving on the road just metres away from the base of the massive concave cooling towers.

"Watch the road to the power station," the site manager advised, "it will be icy."

I set off in his 1.6-litre Ford Sierra GL. It was a very nice car in those days and I felt ten feet tall, driving it. I had travelled less than a mile along the private road from our site to the power station when some large birds on a wet field caught my eye: geese and lots of them.

In those days, I was not as good at bird identification as I am now, and I looked closely to see whether they were greylag geese or rarer white-fronted geese. As I brought my eyes back onto the road in front, I caught sight of a road sweeper for the first time. There was always one on this road. The coal from our site was taken straight to the power station, and the road became very messy with all the lorries travelling between the two places.

The sweeper was about fifty metres ahead of me. I put my foot on the brakes, and the car slid on the ice along the road, rapidly gaining speed down the shallow incline. I tried tooting the horn in vain, hoping the road sweeper might hear me coming and move over to let me pass, there was nothing I could do but sit tight and wait for the inevitable.

SMASH!

I slid right into the rear of the sweeper. The car's bonnet crumpled up, and steam began to issue from the engine. I sat in stunned silence for a few seconds trying to work out how to tell my site manager what I had done to his lovely car.

Before I knew it, the driver of the road sweeper came cautiously alongside.

"You okay young fella?" he inquired in a friendly way.

"Yes, yes I am, thank you," I stuttered, "I'm sorry, I just couldn't stop."

"Been waiting all morning for someone to come sailing into the back of me. The road's like an ice rink."

"It is an ice rink," I said as I gingerly climbed out and joined him, looking at the back of his truck.

"Don't think there's any damage to the truck," he enthused, "pity about your car, it's a bit of a mess."

"I know," I confessed as I looked at the mangled front end of the blue Sierra for the first time, "it's not my car, it's my site manager's."

"Oh dear," was the driver's response.

"Whatever have you done to my car?" Richard asked as he climbed out of a site Land Rover that had brought him to where the car lay in a crumpled heap.

"I slid into the back of the road sweeper," I confessed.

"You must have been driving flat out to do all that damage," he stated in a rather annoyed tone.

"He wasn't," the sweeper driver explained, "it's the ice, you see, treacherous this road is, has been all morning, an accident waiting to happen."

"It has happened," the site manager replied, taking a closer look at the damage I had inflicted on his vehicle.

"Company car is it?" the sweeper driver asked.

"Yes mine," the site manager murmured.

"That's okay then, nothing lost. You either get a new car or get this one fixed up. Simple."

I could see that my site manager was not taking kindly to this verbal barrage.

"Whatever were you doing, Robert? Couldn't you see the sweeper?"

"I could see it," I confessed, "I just couldn't miss it."

"Very slippery," the sweeper driver stated again.

"I can see that," Richard replied as he slipped and grabbed at the remains of the bonnet of his car to remain upright.

Thankfully the damage was repaired, and my escapade was soon forgotten and forgiven.

There are many tragic tales of drivers being distracted while behind the wheel, resulting in terrible accidents. It is so easily done, especially in our day of mobile phones and in-car entertainment. I'm not sure how much the geese played in my unfortunate mishap. They were undoubtedly a distraction; however. It was an important lesson learned to be vigilant at all times, and I often recounted the story in safety seminars I ran years later.

The Bible has some good advice about keeping our eyes on the goal.

Wherefore seeing we also are compassed about with so great a cloud of witnesses, let us lay aside every weight, and the sin which doth so easily beset us, and let us run with patience the race that is set before us, looking unto Jesus the author and finisher of our faith; who for the joy that was set before Him endured the cross, despising the shame, and is set down at the right hand of the throne of God.

(Hebrews Ch12 v1-2)

The writer of these two verses had previously listed men and women of faith who had accomplished great things for God. However, many of them had failed at some point in their lives and some of them on several occasions. Yet these were the cloud of witnesses he spoke of and were examples we can follow. God knows that there will be many distractions which can sidetrack us off our Christian pathway – weights and sins. These can be many and varied, such as hobbies, work, family or friends. Whenever we fail, and however we fail, there is always a way, if we want it to get back on the Christian path and live useful lives for God. The vital thing is to keep *'Looking unto Jesus,'* seeking to please Him in every decision and desire we have.

ABOUT THE AUTHOR

Robert Plant has been interested in wildlife for as long as he can remember. During weeks of school summer holidays at his parent's caravan on the east coast of Yorkshire, he would wander through fields and hedgerows looking for birds, nests and other evidence of wildlife activity. He sought to provide a wildlife haven in his parent's suburban garden long before nest boxes, bird feeders and planting for wildlife were popular.

Robert became a Christian aged sixteen due to the faithful witness of a friend at school. Reading a booklet titled 'Heaven and How to Get There,' Robert was convicted of his sin, got out of bed and kneeling, trusted the Lord Jesus Christ as his Saviour.

After leaving school, he started work in Civil Engineering, becoming the Divisional Safety Manager of a large construction company.

In 1993 Robert felt that God was calling him to preach the Gospel full time, and it soon became apparent that he was gifted to communicate this message to the younger generation. He has travelled extensively across the British Isles, visiting schools and conducting series of children's meetings. He maintains an extensive written ministry for both adults and children.

Robert and his wife Karen have one married daughter and live on the North Antrim Coast of Northern Ireland.

OTHER TITLES BY ROBERT PLANT

Available online or from good Christian bookshops.

TITANIC SHIP OF DREAMS

Tells the remarkable story of John Harper, a preacher on board the ill-fated Titanic with his daughter Nana. After putting Nana into a lifeboat, he walked about the deck, preaching the gospel. Even in the freezing waters of the Atlantic Ocean, he used his last breath to point a passenger to the Lord Jesus.

Age range 8 – 15

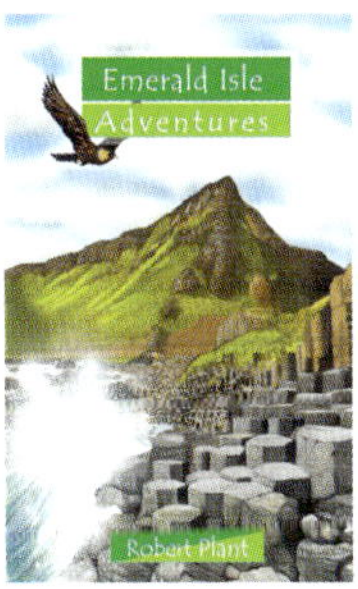

EMERALD ISLE ADVENTURES

Takes readers on an exciting and informative tour around Ireland to discover its rich history, fascinating wildlife and remarkable diversity.

Age range 8 – 15

ESCAPE FROM THE ISLAND OF OCCUPATION

This children's novel recounts how life changed when German forces invaded the Channel Islands. When two children discover a secret, they risk everything to escape to England to tell it.
Age range 8 – 15

RETURN TO THE ISLAND OF OCCUPATION

The sequel to 'Escape' details how two children defy bombs, bullets and submarine attack to return to their island home still under enemy control.
Age range 8 – 15

DISCOVER BRITAIN – SPECTACULAR SHETLAND

Learn about these exciting and unique outlying Scottish Islands in this book, illustrated by the writer's daughter.
Age range 8 – 15

DISCOVER BRITAIN – OUTSTANDING ORKNEY

From Viking invaders to wartime tragedies Scotland's Orkney Islands have a lot to tell.
Age range 8 – 15

HOPE – ANCHOR OF THE SOUL

This unique thirty-one-day, large print publication is written for those passing through various trials. Each day the reader is provided with a few Bible verses and a hymn upon which to meditate.

HAVE YOU CAUGHT THE 3:16?

This short Gospel booklet divides the twenty-five golden words of John Ch3 v16 into ten short phrases with an explanation as to what the verse teaches about God's way of salvation.

HAVE YOU GONE DOWN IN THE 8:36?

Are you a believer in the Lord Jesus Christ? Have you been baptised? This short publication considers ten Scriptural reasons why you should be baptised the Biblical way – by total immersion.

ARE YOU FOLLOWING THE 2:42?

In these days of confusion, does God have a blueprint for Christians to follow on how they gather together? The writer looks at the eight statements of Acts Ch2 v41-42 and seeks to show that God's plan for all Christian meetings and service was laid out soon after the Lord ascended to Heaven.

STRENGTH THAT I SHOULD HOPE

The sequel to 'Hope – Anchor of the Soul,' providing troubled readers with a further thirty-one structured daily readings from God's Word along with a suitable hymn to bring comfort and assurance.